CODE IS FOR HUMANS

BOOK I: THEORY

CODE IS FOR HUMANS

A Guide to Human-Centric
Software Engineering

BOOK I: THEORY

Zohar Jackson

Code Is for Humans
by Zohar Jackson

CodeIsForHumans.com

Independently published
ISBN-13: 9798861816489

This revision date: January 9, 2024
First edition: August 2023
Editor: Liz Wheeler

Contents

Chapter 6: Be a Mensch   119

Chapter 7: Wrapping up Book I   123

Postscript   125

Appendix   126

Preface

About the Book

To write better code and build better products we must understand why engineering and design often fail. Why is it so difficult to write bug-free code? Why do people fail to use products? And why do engineering projects so often go sideways?

The answer to these questions lies in the shortcomings of human cognition and the nature of complexity. This book explores these topics and presents a human-centric approach to software engineering. An approach that considers and compensates for our cognitive biases, cognitive weaknesses, and the chaotic nature of the universe. An approach that teaches how to balance concerns, defend against entropy, take precautions, reduce complexity, and deal with our cognitive shortcomings.

This book is a compilation of what I have learned from decades of writing software, exploring my cognitive abilities, and working with other humans. It is inspired by years of seeing highly intelligent engineers obliviously, and repeatedly, making the same mistakes. They did not understand why things kept breaking. They did not understand why code was constantly needing to be rewritten, and why changes were so expensive. Despite their high IQs, they were simply unable to understand what code is and how it should be written.

Their years of university computer science education had failed them by focusing on algorithms and the theoretical. Valuable knowledge, but not very useful for solving the typical problems engineers face on a daily basis. These graduates were never taught what engineering *is*. What are its fundamental concepts and practices?

The existing programming literature had also failed these engineers by being either too specific, extremist, or just plain wrong. The specific material was concerned with a technique or two, such as a book about object-oriented programming, when much more than a single technique is needed to be a great engineer. These books often did not connect their ideas to an overarching theory or approach to engineering. There was no material that provided engineers with the correct framework for thinking about engineering, while also providing the techniques and tools needed to solve their daily problems. And especially absent from the literature was a discussion about human cognition and its effects on engineering and design. An understanding of the effects, however, is critical to mastering those fields.

I felt engineers needed a book to fill these gaps. This book lays out a framework for understanding what code is and how software should be written. It delineates how code is a tool meant for human minds and meeting human needs. It teaches how humans can reliably describe computations with a complexity far beyond the capabilities of our limited monkey minds. It explains how code can be made human-readable and human-proof. It teaches how to balance concerns, cut the correct corners, defend against entropy, take precautions, reduce complexity, and deal with our cognitive limitations.

This book is the first book of a two-book series. This book, Book I, focuses on the theory of human-centric software engineering, while the second book focuses on the application of the theory. The first book provides theoretical foundations that will be used to explain and support the technical examples and techniques present in the second book. In other words, Book I is idea-heavy, while Book II is code-heavy.

What Is Not Covered in This Book

This book does not cover topics such as algorithms, programming languages, motivational skills, or techniques for navigating corporate politics. These topics have been extensively covered by university courses, self-help books, and the wide range of programming literature available.

Acknowledgments

This book has been distilled from years of experience working on software, my mistakes, and my successes. Credit for many of the ideas in this book must be given to all the great engineers and designers who inspired and taught me. A plethora of books, blogs, comments on Hacker News, Stack Overflow answers, and co-worker's mentoring have all made their way into this book. I thank my teachers, all of whom gave me different pieces of wisdom, and who are too many to name here.

Don Norman's book *The Design of Everyday Things* and John Ousterhout's *A Philosophy of Software Engineering* are two major sources of inspiration that provided me with language and theory that serve as foundations for much of this book. I highly recommend you read them, if you have not done so already.

Introduction

What are we trying to do as software engineers? Most people will answer "Write code and build things!". Yeah, code is nice and all, but *why* do we want to write code and build things? Why do we spend countless hours staring at screens, fighting with debuggers, arguing about syntax, and refactoring code bases?

The most general answer is that we write code to achieve goals. These goals might be financial, emotional, social, or whatever it is that humans desire. The point is we are humans; humans want things, and we use code to get the things we want.

This might seem like an over-reduction of why we write code, but it's not. There are useful ideas we can learn from this reduction. The first idea is that the "goodness of code," or "good code," should be measured by how well the code meets your (or your organization's) goals.

1   Why Code Quality Matters

Code has a strange property, where two programs that have identical functionality can vary by orders of magnitude in performance, maintainability, reliability, and cost. Some code bases will require days to make a simple change, some will require minutes. Some code bases require weeks before a newly on-boarded engineer is able to make a useful contribution. Some code bases are like a haphazard, dirty house of cards. Some are immaculate and strong. The effect of code quality on your ability to achieve your goals is surprisingly large. Even small deficiencies in quality can lead to massive negative outcomes.

With audacity, I will describe this phenomenon as **Jackson's law**:

> *Bad design and engineering cause more harm than you expect,*
> *even when taking into account Jackson's law.*

1

This phrasing is inspired by Hofstadter's law, which states that "It always takes longer than you expect, even when you take into account Hofstadter's Law." Both laws underscore our extreme inability to make predictions about the future.

There are so many expected and unexpected ways that design and engineering can lead to undesirable outcomes. To make matters worse, often the outcomes are non-linear with respect to the design, i.e. small differences in design can result in huge differences in outcomes. Design and engineering interact with the world in a way that is best modeled as a chaotic system. Chapter 3 is dedicated to understanding this phenomenon.

Due to the chaotic nature of code and the large negative outcomes that are likely to occur due to poor engineering, it is critical to study and perfect the art of software engineering. By sharpening your craft, you can reduce and mitigate the chaotic nature of engineering and achieve your goals more easily.

Software engineering is *not* computer science. Computer science is concerned with the time complexity of sorting algorithms, the intricacies of inverting trees, and the theory of computation. Software engineering, on the other hand, has mostly orthogonal concerns. Software engineering is akin to solving a high-dimensional optimization problem where the global maxima is the optimal course of action. A software engineer needs to know how to both navigate and warp the optimization surface to their advantage. They must optimize over a variety of parameters such as system stability, short-term development costs, long-term development costs, upcoming deadlines, cost-of-compute, user satisfaction, user safety, office politics, etc.

There are no pithy programming catchphrases that will provide the optimal solutions to your problem. There are no simple rules to solving the optimization problem that is software engineering. Good judgment is what you need. Unfortunately, judgment is very hard to teach and requires much effort and experience to obtain. In this book, I will try to nudge you toward developing good judgment. I will demonstrate the thought processes that lead to better decisions, I *will* provide pithy phrases that are easy to remember and can be used when navigating the optimization problem. But at the end of the day, it is up to you to put in the work, learn from your mistakes, and think critically about the code you write.

2 Strive for Your Goals, Not "Good Code"

This book is not about writing what people stereotypically call "good code"; it is about writing code that meets your goals. People often have different opinions about what constitutes good code. There are endless fights about conventions, styles, and ideologies. Don't waste your time on that noise. Define your goals and constraints, then figure out what the best code is given those goals and constraints. Focus on the objective and the definition of "good" will follow.

Strive for code that meets your or your organization's goals. Does your organization want code that is cheap to maintain and reliable? Do you want code that is easy to read and understand and doesn't make you want to pull out your hair? Do you need to ship this product by the end of the day no matter what? These, for example, should be the kinds of goals that drive your development choices. Suppose the CEO of Intel is acquiring your startup for 15 billion dollars and gives you an hour's notice of his surprise visit. He is coming to your cubicle to see an impressive demo of what he is buying, but unfortunately, there is nothing all that impressive to show. In this instance, you'll need to write bad code and you need to write it *fast*. This happened to me during the acquisition of Mobileye.

There are no rules in software development that are appropriate in all circumstances. Following "best practices" and advice from pretty blog posts will lead to disaster if they are not filtered with judgment. This type of disaster is often caused by enthusiastic over-engineering, premature optimization, or wasteful perfectionism, topics we will cover later in this book.

Despite all this, striving for goals and not good code is *very* dangerous advice. It is akin to telling people to not follow the law because some laws are immoral. Most laws are, in fact, pretty good, although some do need to be reformed. Similarly, most advice about "good code" is indeed pretty good for most circumstances. It would be rash to start ignoring age-old software wisdom. I am instead encouraging you to start taking advice with a grain of salt, start thinking about why and in what circumstances the advice should be followed, and in what circumstances it should be ignored. This will help you to develop good judgment. Judgment cannot be developed from simply reading, but requires thinking, doing, and experiencing.

Striving for goals instead of code quality will often mislead one to focus on short-term gains at the expense of long-term ones. In these cases, investments in maintainability, reliability, and extensibility are often ignored, which will cause problems in the future. It is therefore absolutely critical to keep long-term costs in mind when defining your goals. In fact, knowing how to properly consider, predict, and mitigate long-term costs is one of the main differentiators of great engineers.

3   Quality Code vs. Good Code

I want to differentiate between this book's usages of the terms "good code" and "quality code." Good code, from this point on, is code that is near optimal for your goals. Quality code is code that is highly readable, maintainable, extensible, and simple. In the platonic world, quality code and good code are identical, but in the real world, where budgets are limited, deadlines are short, and manpower is low, we need to cut corners and make tradeoffs. We need to make decisions based on *context*, and not blindly pursue platonic ideals.

You must accept that not all design decisions can be ideal, not every function beautiful, and not every class polished. In this complex mess of a world, not all your code can be quality, but all your code can be good.

4 What You Will Learn

"Code is for humans" has two meanings. First and foremost, it means that code is a tool for accomplishing human goals. Second, it means that code is a tool for human minds. Code is meant to be written, read, modified, and understood by humans, not machines. We will dive into what the implications of these two meanings are, and I'll teach you how to write code that is optimized for human goals and human minds.

The book will provide concepts, language, mental models, and principles that are critical for developing your craft as an engineer. It will teach you to differentiate and judge, provide you with a language for discussing code and design, and help you determine the best way to meet your and your organization's goals.

5 Terminology

We can start by defining some terms.

As a software engineer, you are producing software that is meant to be used by people. In this book, the term **product** refers to anything you produce—this includes code, documentation, APIs, and schemes, as well as the final executable software. We use the term **user** to refer to the end-users, customers, your fellow engineers, and anybody who will read and interact with your product.

It is important to remember that in this book, co-workers are considered users and the code itself, not just the executable, is considered your product.

System is another term that is used in a non-standard way. In this book, the term is used liberally. All code belongs to a system. A system can be a simple script, a code base, or a complex distributed system. Anytime there are two or more parts interacting, there is a system. A part can consist of a function, a class, a line of code, or a human. The interaction between humans and code is a system: the code is affecting the humans and the humans the code. The term system is a concept, a mental model that is useful when thinking about parts and interactions. There are no hard definitions of where a system starts and ends, or how its components are to be divided. It is up to you to choose whatever is best for the problem at hand.

Usability is a catch-all term used to describe functionality, flexibility, comprehensibility, extensibility, and performance. Usability applies to code just as much as it does to end products.

These somewhat non-standard definitions should not be glossed over. These are definitions that lead to an alternate way of thinking about your users, products, and systems. This alternative way of thinking is absolutely critical to being a great engineer.

Chapter 1

The Human Mind

Instead of imagining that our main task as programmers is to instruct a computer what to do, let us concentrate instead on explaining to human beings what we want a computer to do.
— Donald Knuth

1.1 What Is Code?

When you really think about what code is, it's truly mind-blowing.

Code is a tool for describing computations, also known as programs. And programs, on digital computers, are simply large binary numbers. The space of all possible programs, i.e., the number of possible numbers, is so large that we can't possibly guess the number that we seek, so instead, we write code. A compiler translates our code to a number and thus saves us the trouble of guessing. These are not just any numbers, these are magical numbers. They are like magical spells, because when you zap a rock (a silicon CPU) with the right number, it does what you want it to do. The right magic number will cause a rock to translate natural language, simulate worlds, or have a conversation with you. It is unbelievable!

Why do we need to use code as a tool to arrive at the correct binary number? Why can't we simply write out the number we want and be done with it?

The answer is that our minds are not built for that. We are not capable of coming up with numbers that do what we want. Our minds have evolved and are optimized for an environment of objects, relationships, actions, functions, and natural language. These are the primitives of our thought process; they are what our minds are built for and operate best with.

We operate under the delusion that our minds are general, that they can think and reason about anything. But this is false. In fact, we are a very specialized thinking machine, optimized for our evolutionary environment. We are like an AI that can only play chess. We get around this limitation by turning the whole world into the equivalent of a chessboard. We simplify the complexities of reality into the equivalent of chess pieces. We view reality through simplified abstractions and models.

Much of the difficulty in writing quality code comes from the difficulty of translating the complexities of the universe into the language of our minds. As Martin Fowler said: "Any fool can write code that a computer can understand. Good programmers write code that humans can understand.". Writing code for humans is the equivalent of trying to coerce a specialized chess AI to run general computations. One must translate the complexities of the universe into the language of chess; into the pieces, positions, and movements on the chessboard. Similarly, when describing computations in code, one must use models and abstractions that are compatible with our minds. The higher the compatibility, the better the code will be.

1.2   Code Is for Human Minds

Code is meant to be written, read, modified, and understood by human minds—not computers. It is a common misconception that code is written for computers. It's easy to labor under the illusion of this misconception; after all, code is both written on computers and run on computers. However, the reality is that humans write code, which is then compiled to zeros and ones, which are processed by a machine. If code was for computers, then the machines *would* care what you name your variables or how you abstracted your problem, but they don't. All the silicon cares about are the zeros and ones.

These zeros and ones are called machine language. Below are three functionally equivalent pieces of code, in machine language, assembly language, and Python.

x86 machine language

```
1011100000000111000000000000000000000000000101110110000101000
0000000000000000000000000000000111011000010100001111111110011
0101000000000000000000000000000000000011101000111111100111111
11111111111111111111
```

x86 assembly language

```
mov     eax, 14
mov     ebx, 10
add     eax, ebx
push    eax
push    fmt
call    printf
```

Python

```
print(10+14)
```

Take a moment to look at the three examples and compare how they make you feel. How did the usage of the word "feel" make you feel? A bit surprised I imagine! Feelings are not something you imagined would be discussed in a book about programming. Well, this is not just a book on programming, this is a book about humans programming, and humans have feelings.

I imagine the machine language left you feeling confused, maybe a little frustrated, and maybe the Python made you feel relief. It was obvious to you what the Python was doing, and you probably felt good when you saw it and understood it.

It's clear that the Python is far easier to understand and modify than the assembly, and the assembly is easier than the machine language. The difference in comprehensibility is as extreme as night and day.

The simplicity, beauty, and elegance of the Python should cause your brain to scream out: "This is the way!" Indeed, this **is** the way. What is not obvious is *why* this is the way.

Another example of the non-generality of the brain is presented in Figure 1.1. Despite both sides of the figure containing equivalent information, only the image on the left can be processed by the human brain in a reasonable time frame. The way in which information is presented matters to the brain; not all equivalent information is equivalent to our brains in terms of convenience and comprehension.

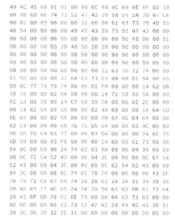

(a) Lion image [28]

(b) A fraction of the hexadecimal representation of the lion image

Figure 1.1: Lion image vs. hex of lion image. Inspired by *Understanding intermediate layers using linear classifier probes* [1].

What is it about our minds that makes the lion image and Python code much easier to understand than hex and binary? What lessons can we extrapolate from these simple examples? We will cover how we can sharpen our ability to discern what the superior code or system design is. I will also show you how to write code that is human-centric and designed for our human brains.

1.3 Humans vs. Computers

To answer these questions, we must first consider the differences between human and computer computation. Below are some of the relevant differences between humans and computers, with a brief description of their consequences as they relate to software engineering.

Humans	Computers	Consequences
Cost tens to hundreds of dollars per hour.	Cost cents to dollars per hour.	Engineers cost orders of magnitude more per hour than computers. Work should be offloaded to computers whenever possible.
Short-term memory of ~10 seconds with max capacity of ~7 items.	Memory remains indefinitely with near unlimited capacity.	Code needs to be written so that engineers do not need to keep many items in their short-term memory to work on the problem.
Small working memory.	Unlimited working memory.	Lines of code should be short. Variable names should be descriptive so that their meaning does not need to be remembered. Required context should be small.
Make mistakes.	Effectively error-free.[1]	Precautions against error should be taken. Tests, designs, and comments should be implemented that protect against human error.
Slow and limited inter-human communication.	Communicate with orders of magnitude higher bandwidth.	Comments should be used to communicate between humans. Code should be written such that other natural language communication such as emails, meetings, and messages are not needed.
Limited capacity for complexity.	Unaffected by complexity, execute whatever they are given.	Code, models and abstractions must be made as simple as possible.
Very lossy inter-human communication.	Communicate with effectively zero loss.	Extra care to communicate clearly must be taken. Knowledge should be communicated in comments and code, not email and messenger apps, so that loss is reduced.

Lossy short- and long-term memory.	All memory is long-term and permanent.	Engineers should not be expected to remember anything, especially not details which are prone to being forgotten or misremembered. Knowledge must be written.
Computation is done using models, abstraction, symbols, and reasoning.	Computation is done using numbers.	Code should be written in the language of the human mind so that it is easy to understand and work on.
Cognitive differences between individuals. Information is processed differently depending on the individual and their current cognitive state.	CPU differences exist, but differences do not result in different end results.	Code should be written for the lowest reasonable denominator. Code should be written so that all the people who will work on it can easily understand it.
Can extrapolate and fill in the blanks.	Follow instructions literally and precisely.	A minor misspecification in code will lead the computer to do the wrong thing, while the same instruction for a human will most likely succeed.

Table 1.1: Humans vs. computers

We will come back to these characteristics of humans and machines, as they provide a foundation and guiding light for many of the engineering principles and practices to come.

1.4   Humans Think Using Abstractions

Often people don't realize the pervasiveness of abstractions in our thinking and conscious experience. There is a joke which describes the situation well.

> There are two young fish swimming along and they happen to meet an older fish swimming the other way, who nods at them and says "Morning, boys. How's the water?" And the two young fish swim on for a bit, and then eventually one

---

[1]Occasionally errors will occur due to cosmic rays and equipment failures.

> of them looks over at the other and goes "What the hell is
> water?"

We live and think in the world of abstractions, yet we hardly realize it.
Humans abstract everything we encounter. We abstract physical objects,
ideas, emotions, and mechanisms. Every entity that has a name is an
abstraction in our minds.

For instance, the word "dog" is an abstraction that we use to categorize
certain four-legged creatures. There is nothing in the physical world that
you can point to and say "This is the physical manifestation of dog," as
dog is only a concept without a physical form. There are instances of
dogs, things which fall into the category of dog, but no dogs themselves.
The word dog is simply a concept we use to help us think, reason, and
make predictions about certain four-legged creatures.

The reason humans use abstractions to think is because we are unable to
store all the details of reality in our working memory. Reality is far too
detailed and complex. We need abstractions to simplify the complexity
of reality into small chunks that can fit in our memory and be usable for
processing.

1.4.1 Models

The title of this section, "Humans think using abstractions," is itself an
abstraction, as it is a simplified explanation for how humans think. In
fact, it is a special type of abstraction called a model.

A **model** is a particular type of abstraction that is used to understand,
analyze, predict, and explain the behavior of a system.

Humans survived and flourished in our evolutionary environment because we were able to create high-quality, predictive models. These
models, for example, enabled us to predict if an animal was a threat or
was planning to attack us. Models of animals enabled us to think about
animals as high-level, unified abstractions rather than as low-level col-
lections of phenomena such as atoms and electrons. Imagine trying to
predict the behavior of a predator by trying to calculate all the future

states of its atoms and electrons. It is an impossible task. Even modern scientists are not capable of predicting animal behavior from the states of an animal's atoms. Instead, scientists use abstractions such as neurons, emotions, and cognitive processes to make predictions.

Models are the building blocks of science. Atoms, for example, are a scientific model. Atoms do not exist in reality; they are merely models in our minds. An atom is the name of a model that enables us to make predictions about certain observed phenomena, such as why photons will sometimes disappear (be absorbed) when they enter certain regions of space (hit an atom), or why some things have mass and take up space.

1.4.2   Not All Models Are of Equal Utility

The quality of one's thinking is highly dependent on the quality of one's models and abstractions. Since models are simplifications and approximations, not all models are of equal utility or predictive value; this is because, inevitably, some information is lost by simplification. What we mean by predictive value is a model's ability to accurately make predictions about observable phenomena.

In 1911, Ernest Rutherford proposed a model of atoms which described a nucleus orbited by electrons. This model was able to account for a number of experimental observations. Bohr came around in 1913 and proposed a new model, which explained more phenomena, including the line spectra of emitted photons. This led the scientific community to discard Rutherford's model and accept Bohr's. Bohr's model was later displaced by the Schrödinger model, which is, again, more complicated but provides more accurate predictions about atomic and electromagnetic phenomena.

Often a perfectly accurate model is not optimal. A more accurate model will often come at the cost of greater complexity. For example, when teaching children about atoms, maybe the Bohr model is more appropriate than the Schrödinger model due to its simplicity and lack of reliance on probability theory.

In mechanical engineering, using Newtonian mechanics and its equations, such as

$$F = MA$$

is usually a much better choice than using the more precise and more complicated Einsteinian equations, which take into account relativity. The increased precision of Einstein's equations is unnecessary for the vast majority of engineering tasks, while the added complexity is likely to lead to human error and even engineering catastrophe.

In general, a model should be as simple as possible while describing the phenomena to the precision that you require. Using a model that is more precise than required, but less simple, will have undesirable consequences and should be avoided.

1.5 Abstractions In Software

Just as models are the building blocks of science, abstractions are the building blocks of software. And just as models need to be simple in order to be useful, so do abstractions.

What does it mean for an abstraction to be simple? Simplicity, in the case of software engineering, is measured by the amount of cognitive load induced by the abstraction. The more "ifs," "thens," "buts," and details of the abstraction, the more that must be kept in one's mind, the more difficult it will be to use the abstraction. A rough way of measuring the cognitive load of an abstraction is to consider how many natural language words are needed to fully describe the abstraction. We can call this measure of complexity **natural language complexity** (NLC), and we will refer to it throughout the book. This measurement of complexity is inspired by **Kolmogorov complexity**, a measure of program complexity that is defined as "the length of the shortest possible description of the string in some fixed universal description language" [23].

This is a rather hard-to-understand definition for those not familiar, and explaining it fully is out of the scope of this book. The basic idea is that we can consider the "string" as the bits output by a program and the "universal description language" as bits that make up the program. Thus the Kolmogorov complexity for a given string is the length of the shortest program that will output said string. To be clear, Kolmogorov complexity is not restricted to bits and computer programs. The universal description language can be a natural language and the computer can be a human or a large language model.

NLC can be viewed as a type of Kolmogorov complexity where the universal description language is limited to the set of natural languages. Thus natural language complexity is the minimum number of natural language words needed to specify a "string" which you can think of as any sequence be it a program, image, or text.

In software, the go-to tools of abstraction are functions, classes, interfaces, variables, components, data structures, conceptual models, and design patterns. In fact, *everything* in software is composed of abstractions. Everything from bits to user interfaces. After all, a bit is just an abstraction of information, a voltage, or a magnetic moment.

Software systems are built from layers upon layers of abstractions. There are the many hardware layers abstracting electrons and atoms into transistors, electrical devices, logic circuits, memory, busses, and computational units. There are the drivers and firmware abstracting the hardware components. There is the operating system layer, which itself has many internal layers of abstraction.

Without these many layers of abstraction writing software such as desktop applications would be insanely time-intensive and expensive. The lesson here is that good abstractions save us time and enable us to accomplish our goals more easily. Abstractions make the impossible possible. A system with the appropriate abstractions will be easy to use, easy to modify, reliable, and efficient.

To excel in software engineering, one must master the art of abstraction.

The process of abstraction consists of conjuring up initial abstraction candidates and then comparing their tradeoffs. The difficulty in abstraction lies both in the conjuring up of good candidates and in comparing their relative costs and benefits. The tradeoffs often include functionality, flexibility, comprehensibility, extensibility, and performance. I use the catch-all term usability to describe these tradeoffs.

There is much to say about abstraction; in fact, much of this book is implicitly about how to design and choose good abstractions. I am assuming you have already studied the basics of abstraction, so we will skip the basics and start with two often ignored topics that are critical to making good abstractions: assumptions and familiarity.

1.5.1 Assumptions

Assumptions are critical to increasing the bandwidth of communication. If communicating parties did not make assumptions, communication would be tediously long and inefficient, as one would have to specify an unreasonable number of details.

The sort() function is an example of an abstraction which uses assumptions to reduce complexity. It is a reasonable assumption that the function will sort alphabetically from A–Z, as this is the default cultural standard for sorting. The function could be named sort_a_to_z() in order to reduce the need for assumptions, but even in that case, there will be assumptions that need to be made, such as the relative sorting order of digits to letters. Specifying the entire sort algorithm in the name is impractical, so we must make do with assumptions. Imagine a sorting function that did not follow the standard sorting assumptions; maybe it sorted non-alphabetically. This type of sorting function would obviously cause endless chaos and bugs for its users.

As an engineer, it is absolutely critical that your users (the people reading your code) will make the same assumptions as you. You must think defensively and consider what your users might assume incorrectly, and take defensive actions such as naming, comments, or re-abstracting so that your assumptions are aligned. This is not a trivial task. It is very hard to know what others know and even harder to know what others will assume. Humans are biased to think that what we know is known by others. This cognitive bias even has a name: **the curse of expertise** or **the curse of knowledge**. You must work hard to unbias your assumptions about other people's knowledge. It is best to err on the side of caution and assume your user does not have as much knowledge as you do. It is better to over-explain than under-explain, to over-simplify than under-simplify.

A great method for reducing incorrect assumptions is to leverage familiarity.

1.5.2   Familiarity

We can leverage the user's prior knowledge by creating abstractions that are similar to those that the user is already familiar with. This enables the user to make valid assumptions about the abstraction without needing to study it in detail. For example, imagine the year is 1940 and you are creating the world's first computer. In 1940, since no one knows what a "computer" is, it makes sense to abstract it as a composition of components such as a screen, keyboard, processor, and memory. In 1940, everyone was already familiar with these terms. People had seen movies, so they knew what screens were, keyboards existed as a part of typewriters, memory was in our minds, and processing was a term in the vernacular. These terms enabled users to make valid assumptions about the objects they represented. Someone would rightly assume that "memory" stores information and that it can be read and written. They'd have intuitively understood that computer screens are for displaying information, and that information on a screen is temporary and changes over time. A key point here is that not only were the names familiar, but the way the items worked was familiar. Using a familiar name for an alien function will cause incredible confusion and should be avoided!

The opposite case, of a familiar function with an unfamiliar name, is less damaging, but still should be avoided. For example, a class named `MessageSender` can safely be assumed to have something to do with sending messages. The user approximately knows what messages are, and knows what sending is, so naming the class with two words that they are already familiar with enables them to quickly make assumptions and get an idea of what it does. If you were to name the class `XDFSender`, the reader is less likely to know that `XDF` is a message type, even if this is incredibly obvious to you. In such a case, adding redundancy and reducing the need for specific knowledge is useful. `XDFMessageSender`, for example, would be a better name. The marginal added verbosity is a price worth paying for the benefit of clarity. Using names that do not assume prior specialized knowledge, and that describe the item in terms of an abstraction the user is already familiar with, is a great way to reduce complexity.

Imagine you wanted to communicate to another engineer the concept of "A robot that enters a room and turns off the light switch." The simplest way to do it would be to use the exact phrase I just used, which has a natural language complexity (NLC) of ten. But let's say you could not use the terms "robot," "light," "switch," or "off" because the engineer was not familiar with these terms or concepts. All of a sudden this becomes a much more daunting task. You must first describe each of these terms conceptually. It is not trivial to describe even what a light switch is; there are so many types of light switches, so many ways of turning them off and on. Without leveraging familiarity, the NLC would jump from ten to thousands or tens of thousands.

This example may seem extreme, but it happens all the time in the real world. Whenever a software engineer invents something new that is unfamiliar, it's the equivalent of inventing a light switch. If you can, you should avoid inventing unfamiliar abstractions, as the harm caused is usually greater than the utility you imagine.

1.5.3 Deceptive Familiarity

I was recently filling my car with fuel and made a mistake while using the pump's keypad, as seen in Figure 1.2.

The pump requested that I enter my zip code and then press enter. Unfortunately, I pressed "Help" instead of "Enter." This caused the system to begin calling the attendant for help. I tried pressing the cancel key to no avail. I had to wait a painful amount of time while the device was ringing, waiting for the attendant to answer, before I could start over and enter my zip code. It was both very annoying and a sign that the system was improperly designed. Why did I press the wrong key?

Figure 1.2: Gas pump keypad

My mind unconsciously modeled this keypad like the numeric keypad on my computer's keyboard (which I use every day). On my keyboard, the bottom right corner is the enter key, so I automatically associated that location with the enter key. To be fair to the designers, this keypad is also similar to a phone keypad. The designers, I imagine, were trying to leverage the user's familiarity with the phone keypad. But they failed when they placed a column to the right of the numbers, as the column indicates a different type of keypad and confuses some users by making them subconsciously think it works like a computer keypad.

If you just thought to yourself that the inconvenience I endured was due to a user error and not a design error, then you are mistaken. All user errors are design errors. We will discuss this further in Chapter 4, and feel free to take a look if you are interested. For now, let's get back to the topic at hand.

The mis-pressed key was caused by a phenomenon I call **deceptive familiarity**. This occurs when assumptions are made about something due to its familiarity, but those assumptions turn out to be false.

A better design, which is not deceptively familiar, would have been for the right row of buttons to be placed as a fifth row instead of as a column. In that case, the "yes" button can be removed as it is redundant with the

Figure 1.3: Numerical keypad on computer keyboard [24]

"Enter/OK" button.

I asked the attendant how often this happens, he shook his head and said "all the time." This is a great example of Jackson's law. A poor design decision made many years in the past is causing a daily nuisance to tens of thousands of gas station attendants and customers around the world.

1.5.4 Object-Oriented Programming

Abstractions and the techniques of abstraction are subject to the laws of natural selection. Great abstractions live long and become widespread, while bad ones disappear and fall out of use.

Object-oriented programming (OOP) is an example of a great abstraction technique. OOP has become extremely popular because it is excellent at reducing complexity at a low cost, i.e., it has minimal downsides. The reason why OOP is so successful at reducing complexity is because it abstracts computations in the natural language of our minds—the language of objects, attributes, and actions. It leverages familiarity and common assumptions to reduce complexity.

As an example of this, nearly every introduction to OOP starts by explaining how OOP can be used to model an animal, often a dog. A dog is seamlessly modeled with a `Dog` class and `bark()` method. The dog can be modeled with objects and actions which are part of the environment our brains were naturally selected for, concepts we are familiar with and can make reasonable assumptions about.

1.5.5   To Be Continued

As an engineer, it is your job to use the various tools of abstraction, such as functions, classes, interfaces, variables, components, data structures, conceptual models, and design patterns to reduce complexity.

There is much more to say about creating great abstractions, but let's hold off for now and continue on the topic of the mind and discuss the engineer's greatest foe—cognitive load.

Chapter 2

Cognitive Load and Complexity

Complexity is the engineer's enemy number one. There is nothing that causes more harm and gets more in the way of your goals than complexity. Complexity induces cognitive load, and cognitive load impedes the writing of functioning code and completing tasks. Complexity is the leading cause of bugs, it's why progress slows, heads hurt, and projects fail. Knowing how to minimize complexity is the most important skill to master as a software engineer. If you learn to be proficient at it, you will be an exceptional engineer.

2.1   What Are Complexity and Cognitive Load?

There are multiple types of complexity, Kolmogorov complexity, self-dissimilarity, time complexity, and more. But when we talk about complexity in terms of software engineering (*not* computer science), we mean something different. In software engineering, complexity is best measured in terms of its effect on the mind. Complexity is the amount of cognitive load that is induced when trying to understand, maintain, and extend a program or system. To be more precise and differentiate between other types of complexity, we can call this **cognitive complexity**. Cognitive complexity can be measured per individual, or as a distribution over a population. The distinction is made because different people will have different amounts of cognitive load from the same unit of code. Some people will find certain abstractions and syntax easier to understand than others. Unless stated otherwise, in this book, when I use the term complexity, I mean cognitive complexity.

Natural language complexity is a reasonable approximation of cognitive complexity when used to measure the complexity of models and architectures. It is less useful when measuring the complexity of specific units of code, such as statements or functions. One of the reasons for this is that a unit of code can be obfuscated through unclear symbols and syntax, which are not accounted for by NLC. For example, a statement with information-less variable names, such as x1, x2, x3, and x4 would have the same NLC as the same statement with names like `velocity`, `x_position`, `y_position`, and `acceleration`. Clearly, the latter is less confusing and induces less cognitive load.

NLC also fails when the variable names are not just information-less but are counter-intuitive. For example, the code `fish.bark()` can be described as a statement calling the bark function on the fish object and has an NLC of 10. In contrast, the statement `dog.bark()` has the same NLC but causes less confusion. A dog barking is a familiar idea and is not a surprising method in a dog class, whereas a fish barking is quite strange and additional memory must be used to remember why this fish instance is barking, and what the bark actually means. Maybe the engineer must remember that this is not a fish, and is really a `Furry, Incognito, Small, Husky (FISH)`, or maybe a "bark" is some type of swimming maneuver. The additional memory that must be used to remember why a fish is barking acts as a drain on our cognition and reduces our cognitive capabilities. Cognitive load theory explains how our usage of memory affects our cognition.

2.2 Cognitive Load Theory

Cognitive load theory provides a model of how human brains learn, process, and store information. The theory suggests that learning and thinking happen best when information is structured and presented in a way that is aligned with the human cognitive architecture. The theory is based on widely accepted theories of cognition, primarily:

1. Human memory is composed of working memory and long-term memory.

2. Information must be stored in long-term memory in the form of schemas.

3. Processing new information induces load on working memory, which degrades the learning process.

The schema is cognitive load theory's term for what we have been calling abstractions. In cognitive load theory, cognitive load is measured in terms of the amount of working memory used. The more working memory used, the higher the cognitive load. Psychologists have measured the capacity of working memory and determined that it is limited to about five (plus or minus three) units of information, commonly referred to as "chunks." A **chunk** is a unit of information that the brain can store and retrieve as a single entity. Chunks can consist of individual pieces of information, or they can be more complex and consist of multiple pieces of related information that are compressed into a single unit.

In the US, we use chunking as a tool for communicating and remembering phone numbers. The ten digits that comprise a US phone number are always chunked into three units of information. The phone number 5355255511 is written as 535-525-5511. Remembering a phone number consisting of three chunks is far easier than remembering ten un-chunked digits.

An experiment by George A. Miller in 1954 demonstrates the extreme power of chunking. In his experiment, people were trained to remember a series of binary digits. He taught the participants to group the digits into groups of five, recode the group into a name ("twenty-three" for 10111), and remember the names. Using this strategy, participants were able to remember as many as forty binary digits. Remembering forty ones and zeros sounds remarkable, and it certainly would be if the participants actually remembered ones and zeros, but they didn't. All they had to do was remember eight numbers (eight chunks), where each chunk was the decimal equivalent of five binary digits.

We can understand this technique as taking advantage of compression and familiarity. The participants were able to compress five binary digits into a number between 0 and 31 [1]. Note that I wrote a "number" and not "two decimal digits." Participants remembered "twenty-three," not "two three." This is because participants were familiar with the number twenty-three—they already had a schema for it in their minds and simply needed to store that schema in their working memory, instead of two schemas, such as "two" and "three."

2.2.1 Insights from Machine Learning

My personal model for understanding schemas and working memory is inspired by machine learning and latent spaces.

In machine learning, there is the concept of latent space. The latent space is the space of all possible points that can be represented by a model. In neural network approaches, the network learns to represent information as a point, a coordinate, in the multidimensional latent space. For instance, in a 4-dimensional latent space, a network may represent the concept of dogs at point (5, 3, 100, 4). Cats, which are kind of similar (all things considered), may be located nearby at point (5.2, 3, 101, 2.7). Generally, nearby points represent similar things.

My model of human cognition understands units of working memory as only being capable of holding latent space coordinates. One unit of memory can hold one latent space coordinate. In machine learning, a point in latent space can represent anything: it can be a digit, a concept, or an image. It is the weights and connections of the network that determine what that point represents. Learning is, thus, the process of finding a point in latent space that is best suited to represent that entity, and then adjusting the network's weights such that the point is interpreted as an accurate representation of the entity. The coordinate serves as a compressed representation of the entity, and training attempts to minimize the lossy-ness of both the compression and decompression.

In humans, I think a similar mechanism is in operation. Learning can be understood as the process of finding the right coordinate and modifying our neural connections to interpret that coordinate in the correct way.

---

[1]Five binary digits (bits) can represent up to 32 different values.

Learning things we are already familiar with is relatively easier because our brain knows how to interpret and work with that region of the latent space (nearby coordinates). The learner can leverage past learning, and not need to expend the effort of learning everything from scratch.

Sometimes an entity cannot be compressed to a single point, and will instead require multiple points. This can occur when an entity is too complex, has too many details, the learner is incapable of finding an optimal model, or the entity is too foreign to the learner's latent space. Since an entity consisting of multiple points requires multiple chunks of working memory, additional cognitive load is induced.

Regardless of the biological accuracy of the above model, it is a useful model for thinking about cognition for the purposes of software engineering.

2.2.2 Types of Cognitive Load

Cognitive load theory breaks down cognitive load into three types: intrinsic cognitive load, extraneous cognitive load, and germane cognitive load.

Intrinsic cognitive load is the inherent difficulty of the material itself, which is partially influenced by prior knowledge of the material. This can approximately be thought of as the minimum number of chunks the material can be compressed to, or its intrinsic complexity.

Extraneous cognitive load refers to the way a topic is presented, and is often used to describe unnecessary cognitive load. This can be due to obfuscation, sub-optimal abstraction, or any presentation that impinges on cognition.

Germane cognitive load is the amount of mental effort required to process and learn new information. This load can be affected by factors such as the complexity of the material, the learner's prior knowledge, and the learner's motivation. In cognitive overload theory, information can only be stored in "schemas," and thus, germane cognitive load is the load that occurs when creating schemas.

2.2.3   Cognitive Overload

Cognitive overload occurs when working memory is exhausted by any combination of the three cognitive loads described above. High cognitive load leads to poor performance on tasks, reduced accuracy, and decreased speed. When people are working under high cognitive load conditions, errors and mistakes are likely to occur. In software development, the existence of bugs is strong evidence that the complexity, and thus the cognitive load induced by the code, is too high.

In order to prevent cognitive overload, an engineer should design their software in a way such that all three types of cognitive load are minimized.

Ideally, the writer of the code should take the burden of cognitive load on him or herself so that the cognitive load of the user (another engineer or end-user) is minimized. Taking the burden of cognitive load means expending extra effort to make sure the code is less complex. The reason the load should be shifted to the writer of the code is because engineering is not a zero-sum game. Code is read and run orders of magnitude more times than it is written. Thus, one person expending additional effort once (when writing the code) results in hundreds of people expending less effort multiple times (when using the code).

One of the reasons Jackson's law holds true is because of this asymmetry. Bad code will be read and run orders of magnitude more times than it is written, causing the harm to occur far more times than is needed.

The same scaling phenomenon does not only apply to code, but to any easily replicated item, such as songs, cars, books, and courses. There are some sub-par Beatles songs that were written and recorded in a few hours that have now been listened to *billions* of times all over the world. Think about how much more joy would have been brought to the world if the Beatles would have invested a bit more time and energy into producing those songs.

This phenomenon is called the **scale law of returns**. The scale law of returns states that the return on investment for products that reach large scales is outsized. When a product is widely distributed, the value of each improvement (each investment) should be multiplied by the scale of the product in order to calculate the total return.

$$return = value \times scale$$

The three variables in this equation should be interpreted liberally. Scale can be the number of users, the number of times a unit of code is run, the number of usages, or the number of widgets produced. Value and return can be in units of monetary value, emotional value, or ethical value.

Finally, the scale law of returns does not indicate who receives the returns. Sometimes, the benefits of the investment are returned to the investor, sometimes to the users, but more often than not, both parties benefit. In the case of widely distributed products, it is important to keep in mind the outsized benefit of additional effort and invest accordingly.

2.3   Recognizing complexity

There are two heuristics that can be used as a first pass to recognize complexity.

1. If something is hard to understand, it is complex.

2. If something is hard to modify, maintain, or extend, it is complex.

These heuristics are useful but they do not work in all cases. For example, often something is easy to understand for one person and not for another. What do we do then? Is the item complex or not? The best way to alleviate this problem is to understand the cognitive biases that affect our recognition of complexity. There are four biases that get in the way of recognizing complexity: producer bias, the curse of cognition, the curse of knowledge, and self-serving bias.

2.3.1   Producer's Bias

Recognizing complexity is particularly hard if you are the producer of the complexity. **Producer's bias** is a cognitive bias which refers to the phenomenon of individuals underestimating the complexity of products they themselves have produced. This bias is easily observed by comparing the difficulty you have in understanding code you wrote, versus code written by others. Everyone's code looks better to themselves than it does to someone else. If you think the code you wrote is of complexity X, then it is probably of complexity 1.5X to anyone else who will read it.

Producer's bias is a result of a lack of familiarity, underestimation of cognitive differences between individuals (known as the curse of cognition), and underestimating the background information needed (known as the curse of knowledge). Familiarity, our old friend, rears its head here for obvious reasons. The person who wrote the code has spent much time thinking about it, working on it, and understanding it. Things we understand well, are generally no longer complicated or incur a high cognitive load. The producer has already developed a schema for the code and does not incur germane cognitive load when thinking about it. This lack of germane cognitive load biases the producer into thinking that the code is objectively low in complexity.

2.3.2   The Curse of Cognition

The curse of cognition occurs when a person underestimates the cognitive differences between individuals; when they assume others have similar mental processes, cognitive strengths, and weaknesses as themselves. This underestimation of cognitive differences between individuals is a major source of error in the estimation of code complexity.

In software engineering, the curse of cognition often appears as differences in short-term memory or ability to comprehend certain concepts and designs. Your fellow engineer might be a genius, but they may have a very poor short-term memory. Intelligence is not scalar, but rather vector, i.e., there is a direction to it. One can be a genius at one thing and an idiot at everything else. Consider yourself, and you will realize that there are many things that you are totally incompetent at, which come effortlessly to others. Often these differences are not due to a lack of practice, but rather a difference in innate ability or possibly in deeply established, learned cognitive algorithms.

In addition to differences in innate abilities, people process information in surprisingly different ways. For example, some people hear words in their heads when reading (subvocalization), and some people do not. Both sides are usually shocked when they discover that other people don't experience reading in the same way.

As it relates to software engineering, some engineers are very comfortable thinking about recursion, whereas others find it difficult. Some engineers are more comfortable with OOP, while others prefer functional programming.

Of all the cognitive differences between individuals, in my experience, the differences in short-term memory cause the most damage. Some engineers have outstanding short-term memories and are able to keep track of the meaning and details of many entities, and thus tend to skimp on descriptive names, simple abstractions, and comments. Their code is then impossible to understand to the typical engineer. Usually, these people with strong short-term memories are considered "geniuses," which leads to the phenomenon of "geniuses" often writing impossible-to-understand code.

2.3.3   The Curse of Knowledge

The curse of knowledge is a bias that occurs when one assumes that other individuals have the background knowledge needed to understand the information at hand. We've all had the experience where a knowledgeable person will talk to us and incorrectly assume we have the background knowledge needed to understand them. In cases like this, the individual is mostly incomprehensible. The same phenomenon happens in software when assuming a user knows certain acronyms, project-specific details, or tricks of the programming language.

The curse of knowledge caused so many problems at SpaceX that Elon Musk sent a company-wide email stating that the "excessive use of made-up acronyms is a significant impediment to communication" and banned the usage of all acronyms that were not personally approved by himself.

2.3.4   Self-Serving Bias

The **self-serving bias** is a cognitive bias that distorts our perception in a way that "maintains or enhances self-esteem, or the tendency to perceive oneself in an overly favorable manner." [14]

This bias causes engineers to overestimate their abilities and the quality of their code. It is more emotionally pleasant to think of our code as great and ourselves as great engineers than to be self-critical. This is a learned bias, as it is partially the result of a reinforcement learning process driven by the pleasure of self-serving thoughts. Self-serving thoughts, after all, are pleasurable, so we are reinforced to do more and more of that type of thinking.

2.3.5   Lowest Reasonable Denominator Code

We all are influenced by the above biases to varying degrees. Worse still, we are mostly blind to the biases; we rarely notice when we are being biased.

Due to their pervasiveness and ill effect, you must work extra hard to unbias your estimations of the complexity and quality of your code. Without actively unbiasing your estimations, your code will be much worse than you think it is.

One approach to reducing the effects of these biases is to intentionally write code for everyone, designed for the **lowest reasonable denominator** (LRD) of cognitive abilities, skills, and knowledge. This allows you to not have to constantly consider whether the people reading your code know what X is or understand how Y works. Instead, just write it for idiots—write code for the LRD.

When communicating with someone, and especially when teaching, it is imperative to build a model of what the other person knows and what they don't know. How they think and how they don't think. Without that model, you will either be communicating at too high or too low of a level. All good teachers and communicators do this.

Writing code is a lot like teaching. In fact, for the purposes of computation (i.e. what the code does), code should be written so as to teach the reader what it is doing and why it is doing it. Code should read like a teaching lesson.

In order to write the lesson, you need to know what your student (user) already knows. Sometimes engineers think "I know only my co-worker X will read this code. I will write it for their skill level and knowledge." This approach rarely makes sense, as it runs the risk of incorrectly estimating your co-worker's knowledge and abilities, in addition to being wrong about who in the unpredictable future may end up using the code. Thus, the safest way to model your user is to imagine them as the abstract lowest reasonably denominated user.

In Book II, we will discuss concrete approaches to writing lowest reasonable denominator code. For now, let's continue with the theory that stands behind these concrete approaches.

2.4 How to Reduce Complexity

Countless evangelists preach their opinions and approaches to writing good code. Some preach functional programming, others preach object-oriented programming. Some preach extensive usage of comments, others preach comment-free code. The list of opposing techniques goes on and on. What are we to make of these contradictory claims? How can smart, talented people promote opposite approaches? In my opinion, the differences are topical. All approaches are trying to achieve the same thing; they are all trying to reduce complexity. Despite their differences, all the approaches for reducing complexity are based on one basic principle: **make information easier to place into working memory**. This means two things: one, making information simpler so that it can be compressed into fewer and simpler chunks, and two, making the process of loading information into memory easier. The term "information" is used here liberally to refer to any fact, detail, entity, or concept.

All methods of complexity reduction are based on only four techniques:

1. Reduce information

2. Hide information

3. Explain information

4. Compartmentalize information

2.4.1   Technique 1: Reduce information

Every bit of information has a cost. Every feature, parameter, class, and dependency increases the overall complexity of a code base. The more that can be removed, the better. In the case of multiple functions, this does not mean removing a function and placing its code into another existing function. That is just moving, not removing. Instead, it means removing the functionality provided by a function. Is this function really necessary? Is there a way to organize the data or the system so that this code is no longer needed?

When discussing engineering at SpaceX, Elon Musk famously said, "The best part is no part... It weighs nothing, costs nothing, can't go wrong... Undesigning is the best thing. Just delete it." The same principle holds true for software. Besides increasing the resilience of the system, reducing information reduces the cognitive load of working with the code. The fewer features, functions, flows, and dependencies, the fewer things one must hold in one's working memory, and the less likely one is to make mistakes when working on the code.

Every detail, condition, and gotcha of a code base is information that has a cost. Whether it's a so-called "small detail" or "big detail," it still requires one (or more) chunks of working memory. And working memory is a precious resource that needs to be conserved.

Look at the JavaScript truth table in Figure 2.1 for the == operator. This table describes the result of comparing an item in a column to an item in a row by the == operator. The amount of gotchas and details in the table is far too much to be easily chunked into a single chunk. The complexity of this operator leads to many bugs. It's so bad that the accepted best practice is to never use the operator and simply to use the ===, which is a far less particular, and more predictable, operator.

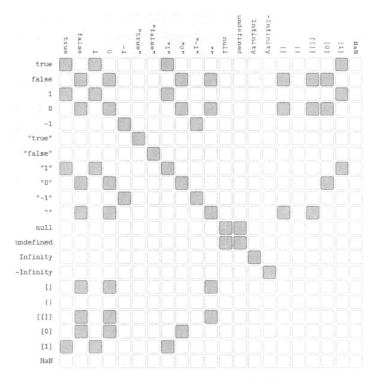

Figure 2.1: Javascript truth table [3]

The reason this operator appears so complicated is because you don't have a schema that accounts for all the details and exceptions. And making this schema is not a trivial task.

In Figure 2.2 is a classic XKCD comic making fun of this similarly complex behavior.

Figure 2.2: XKCD Types #1537

2.4.2   Technique 2: Hide information

When information can't be reduced, then we can do the next best thing and hide it. All unnecessary details should be hidden from the user. Interfaces, abstractions, classes, and functions are examples of tools that are used to hide information. Information hiding can also be visual, such as the folding of code in an editor.

As Yossi Kreinin wrote: "In code and in many kinds of text, a large part of readability is the ability to not read most of it, to quickly learn where to look and what to skip. A big point of structured programming or modules is the not-read ability they provide." [8] As an engineer, you should try to make your code as "not-readable" as possible.

Encapsulation, one of the key ideas of object-oriented programming, is all about information hiding. Encapsulation hides information in classes using private members and methods, and only exposes a fraction of the total information through its public interfaces. The implementation details of the internals of the class are hidden from any users of that class, thus saving them much cognitive load.

Another way to hide information is through internal system design. Information in interfaces can be hidden by manipulating the design of the system internals. Designs can be chosen so that less information is needed by the user, as things are done automatically behind the scenes.

Car transmissions are a good example of this. The automation of the transmission in automatic transmission vehicles enables the hiding of which gear is currently selected from the user, whereas in a manual transmission vehicle, it is imperative that the user knows which gear is currently selected. A great engineer will choose a design that allows more information to be hidden from the user. This is equivalent to choosing to design a car with an automatic instead of a manual transmission. It is important to remember that the complexity of your interfaces is highly dependent on the design of the internals. A stick shift and clutch is a much more complex interface than a simple gear selector.

The filesystem is a superbly designed abstraction that hides information and leverages familiarity. A file is implemented as a record that points to a number of fragments of bits located at various locations on a user's hard drive. But this is not how the interface is designed. Instead, a filesystem provides users with a simple interface consisting of a few operations such as create, move, delete, and rename. This interface totally hides the complexities of file fragmentation from the user. A file is named "file,", rather than "collection of bits" or some more accurate technical name, because the technical implementation details implied by a more accurate name are not needed for the user and would only increase their cognitive load.

The system was designed such that a simple interface could be used. It was designed so that it mirrored real-world physical files and was familiar to the users. It was designed so that the name itself, "file," explained the functionality and conceptual model of the system (technique #3).

2.4.3   Technique 3: Explain information

Explaining information reduces germane cognitive load and the effects of the curse of knowledge bias, and reduces the likelihood of incorrect assumptions.

Naming is probably the most important tool used to explain information in software engineering. An entity named in a way that describes exactly the information it contains and its functionality provides a very quick and convenient explanation of the entity. If a name cannot be chosen in a way that explains the entity, then it is often a sign that the entity should be split into multiple entities, or abstracted differently. Names should leverage familiarity so that the user knows what the item is without needing to look too deeply into it.

Familiarity, after all, is effectively a way to explain information. Familiarity is about explaining information in terms of other information; it is about creating symbolic links in people's minds. Creating a symbolic link induces much less cognitive load than learning a schema from scratch, just as creating a symbolic link on a filesystem is a much cheaper operation than creating all the bits of a file from scratch.

Of course, beyond naming and familiarity, there are standard tools available for explaining information such as comments, documentation, diagrams, and videos. These should be used as secondary tools after the limits of naming and familiarity have been reached.

2.4.4   Technique 4: Compartmentalize

Compartmentalizing information in software engineering is of utmost importance as it plays a crucial role in managing complexity and reducing cognitive load. The goal of compartmentalization is to divide information in a way such that each division, each compartment, can be contained in a single chunk of memory.

Abstractions, components, variables, functions, and even lines of code are examples of compartments. Compartmentalizing is about choosing lines of demarcation such that each division contains an amount of information that is easily compressible to a single chunk.

Information theory defines information in terms of probabilities: the more something is a surprise, i.e., the less probable it is to occur, the more informative it is. In other words, the more surprising something is, the more information is needed to represent it. The more information, the more cognitive load. If we look back at the JavaScript == operator, we notice that its dynamics are surprising. It requires a large table to describe. The lesson here is that reducing the amount of surprise increases compressibility. And thus, in order for a unit of information to be chunkable, it must contain a limited amount of surprising information.

2.5 Complexity Is Not Inherently a Problem

To be clear, complexity is not inherently detrimental to a system's operation. There is nothing wrong with complex systems. There are tons of complex systems that work really well. For example, the human body is an *extremely* complex system, and overall it works very well. Nature, DNA, and cellular biology are all super-complex systems that work very well. In fact, arguments can be made that the complexity of certain biological systems adds to their resilience. For example, having many pathways for doing the same thing adds redundancy in the case of fighting pathogens and disease.

The problem with complexity and complex systems is that they cannot be understood by us, by our minds. Our minds cannot keep track of all the details of complex systems. Complex systems are mostly in-compressible. They resist simplification, and thus cannot fit into our working memory. And anything that cannot be fit into working memory cannot be understood. The complexity of biology, for example, is why the progress of biological research is so slow and difficult.

2.6   Theoretical Knowledge Is Not Enough

Knowing that complexity and cognitive load are the primary sources of bugs, and knowing the high-level techniques for reducing them, are not enough to become proficient at writing low-complexity code. In order to obtain the skills, and not just the theoretical knowledge, you must have the right approach.

When you find a bug, ask yourself: Why did it happen? Was it due to cognitive overload? Which of the principles above could have been used to prevent this error? You may not know how the complexity can be reduced, but that does not mean that it cannot be. Ask a talented co-worker for their thoughts, and they will most likely point out something you missed. Learn from bugs, as they are super-valuable lessons. Retrospection is key if you want to level up your skills.

2.6.1   Be a Complexity Extremist

In addition to retrospection, you need to be proactive. Engineers tend to be very heavily biased toward underestimating the costs of complexity. You need to counteract the bias by being an extremist. If you see something that is slightly more complex than it needs to be, spend some time figuring out how to simplify it—fix it. Even if it's a small improvement, it's nearly always worth it. Complexity adds up, such that the whole is greater than the sum of its parts. Small improvements have a similarly outsized effect, making them more valuable than they appear.

Unless energy is constantly spent to counteract the forces of complexity, it will creep up and destroy your code base. Spend extra time designing your abstractions. Invest in occasional refactorings and cleanups. Don't let minor complexities creep through your code reviews: fight them at every step.

People who really grasp the importance of simplification can sometimes be seen as zealots. But let me assure you, anti-complexity extremists are not really extremists. Rather, they are moderates that only appear to have an extreme view to the average engineer. That is because the average engineer is not aware of the true cost of complexity. Of course, you should be an extremist within reason. An extreme extremist will cause more harm than good. You will get stuck perfecting code instead of making progress. It is important that your goals are not lost to extreme extremism. In Chapter 5, we talk about balancing concerns, perfection versus progress, and the appropriate level of extremism in regard to complexity.

Chapter 3

Jackson's Law

> Bad design and engineering cause more harm than you expect, even
> when taking into account Jackson's law.
> — Zohar Jackson

When we talk about the design and engineering of software, we are
referring to multiple things. These include the design of the code, user
interfaces, APIs, command-line arguments, and graphical user interfaces.
Variable names, abstractions, and conceptual models also fall into this
milieu. It includes the defensive mechanisms that prevent user errors and
the corrective feedback mechanisms when they inevitably, nonetheless,
err. In fact, every expression, every statement, every character, and every
indentation in a code base should be considered part of the overall design.

As engineers, we see firsthand how bad design and engineering of our
code bases affects our productivity, but we are less aware of its effects on
others. We are mostly blind to our users' experiences and frustrations
when using our products. Feedback loops are rarely in place to properly
inform engineers of their users' experiences. Consider all the products
you have purchased that have something annoyingly wrong with them.
Backpacks, wireless mice, cars, etc. Do you contact the designers and
let them know where they erred and how much that error harms you?
Probably not. The designer's blindness to the user's experience occurs
not just for software products but for all products, including physical
items, laws, social systems, incentives, and regulations.

By increasing our awareness of the detrimental consequences resulting
from bad design and engineering, and gaining insight into the factors
behind these negative outcomes, we can develop improved products and
create a more beautiful world.

3.1   Minor Complexities Count

A small leak will sink a great ship.

— Benjamin Franklin

A common misconception amongst engineers is that minor complexities do not cause problems; that minor complexities somehow don't add to the overall complexity of the system. In the process of giving code reviews, I often request of the authoring engineer that they improve the naming of a variable. Sometimes the engineer will respond with the following sentiment: "Yes the name could be more clear but it's kinda obvious what it is given the context. The user will figure it out. Anyway, it's just a variable name!"

This reasoning is wrong. The nature of cognitive load is such that once the mind is overloaded, cognitive performance falls off a cliff. We only have six or so working memory slots in our minds, and it is, thus, imperative to keep them available for the complicated parts of the code that cannot be simplified away. If a variable is named correctly, it does not require the use of any working memory, as upon seeing the name one instantly knows what the variable does. The variable is thus "simplified away." A seemingly "minor complexity," in this example a non-descriptive variable name, still uses one slot of precious memory, thus making it not really minor. There is no such thing as a minor complexity.

In some languages, there are types named i32 and f32. This convention is not that complicated; it's pretty trivial to understand that i32 is a 32-bit integer type and f32 is a 32-bit floating type. But notice that we have to say it explicitly—we have to explain what the type is. There is some translation going on in our minds, some cognitive load. If the types were named int32 and float32 there would be no translation necessary. Maybe if you are familiar with one of the languages, the translation is not necessary, but it is definitely necessary for some engineers and, as discussed, code should be written for the lowest reasonably denominated engineer.

Designers need to be extremists about reducing cognitive load, and should act as if there is no such thing as a minor complexity. One slot of precious memory should not be treated as minor.

As XKCD correctly points out in Figure 3.1, one `goto` statement, a minor complexity, can lead to being attacked by a dinosaur.

Figure 3.1: XKCD GOTO #292

3.2 Chaotic Systems

A chaotic system is a type of system that is very sensitive to initial conditions and small changes. Small changes can lead to significantly different outcomes. Chaotic systems are characterized by complex and unpredictable behavior, which is often perceived as random. Of course, the behavior is often not actually random; rather, it is too complex for us to understand, so we perceive it as unpredictable and, thus, random.

Regrettably, both code and design are chaotic in nature, whereby even minor alterations can yield drastically different and difficult-to-anticipate results.

Chaotic systems are **non-linear**, in the sense that the magnitude of the result of a change is not linearly related to the magnitude of the change. A little change in a design can lead to a huge improvement in the utility of the product, or alternatively, make the product completely useless. A small typo can lead to a bug that causes a customer to cancel a billion-dollar contract. A semicolon in the wrong place or an off-by-one error can lead to an aircraft crashing and hundreds of deaths.

Chaotic systems are often **non-continuous**, meaning that the effects of changes on a system are not smooth. For example, a change may have no effect on a system, but then once it reaches a critical threshold, the system collapses. This is the case in the classic proverb of the straw that broke the camel's back. It is impossible to predict which straw it's going to be, but you can predict that eventually, the back will break if you keep placing straws on it.

An example of the non-linear and non-continuous nature of design is the design of nuclear weapons protocols. If the protocol fails, even by a little bit, the outcome is not a little bit of destruction—the outcome is nuclear war, billions of people dead, and possibly the extinction of humankind.

There have been a number of cases in history, wherein the design of protocols around nuclear weapons have either saved or almost destroyed the world. There was an incident during the Cuban Missile Crisis in which a Soviet submarine believed that it was being attacked, and that nuclear war had started. Captain Valentin Savitsky decided to launch the onboard nuclear missiles. Protocol dictated the approval of two other officers besides the captain. The political officer onboard approved the strike, but Vasily Arkhipov, a lower-level officer, blocked it—thus averting nuclear war. The designers of the protocol saved the world by requiring three, instead of two, officers to approve the use of nuclear weapons.

Our minds are limited, and cannot consider all the ways things can go wrong or how much harm can be incurred from each misdesign. We suffer from **possibility bias**, which is the tendency to overestimate the number and likelihood of positive or neutral possible outcomes and underestimate the number and likelihood of negative outcomes. Possibility bias is related to the nature of the universe, and the laws of entropy. There are simply so many more ways for things to go wrong than for things to go right. There are so many more ways to break something than build something. Possibility bias is closely related to **optimism bias**, which is the tendency for individuals to believe that they are less likely to experience negative events and more likely to experience positive events compared to others.

3.3   The Effects of a Design Are Hard to Predict

The effects of a design are hard to predict. Even when you consider the design thoroughly, there will inevitably be outcomes that you were unable to predict. In *Thinking in Systems* the following story is told.

> Near Amsterdam there is a suburb of single-family houses
> all built at the same time, all alike. Well, nearly alike. For
> unknown reasons it happened that some of the houses were
> built with the electric meter down in the basement. In other
> houses the electric meter was installed in the front hall. These
> were the sort of electric meters that have a glass bubble with a
> small horizontal metal wheel inside. As the household uses
> more electricity, the wheel turns faster and a dial adds up
> the accumulated kilowatt-hours. During the oil embargo and
> energy crisis of the early 1970s the Dutch began to pay close
> attention to their energy use. It was discovered that some of
> the houses in this subdivision used one-third less electricity
> than the other houses. No one could explain this. All houses
> were charged the same price for electricity, all contained simi-
> lar families. The difference, it turned out, was in the position
> of the electric meter. The families with high electricity use
> were the ones with the meter in the basement, where people
> rarely saw it. The ones with low use had the meter in the front
> hall where people passed many times a day the little wheel
> turning around, adding up the monthly electricity bill. [10]

Who could have predicted the huge effect design had on gas consump-
tion? I don't think anyone could have predicted it. It is precisely because
prediction is so difficult that it is imperative to follow the best practices of
design and engineering. Best practices enable you to make good choices
without needing to make good predictions.

3.4   Scale Effects

In Chapter 2, we discussed the scale law of returns and noted how when
a product is produced in volume or has a large number of users, the
return on investment is outsized. This phenomenon occurs due to the
multiplicative effects of scale. The same multiplicative effects are relevant
to Jackson's law.

A poor design will cause a little harm to one user but a lot of harm when you multiply it by millions of users. Of course, the same is true in reverse; a small improvement to a design can have an outsized benefit.

One of the reasons we underestimate these effects is due to **scope insensitivity**. Scope insensitivity is a cognitive bias that occurs "when the valuation of a problem is not valued with a multiplicative relationship to its size" [25]. Wikipedia contains the following example of scope insensitivity article:

> In one study, respondents were asked how much they were willing to pay to prevent migrating birds from drowning in uncovered oil ponds by covering the oil ponds with protective nets. Subjects were told that either 2,000, or 20,000, or 200,000 migrating birds were affected annually, for which subjects reported they were willing to pay $80, $78 and $88 respectively. [25]

Another phenomenon that occurs at scale is the occurrence of the improbable. Low-probability events are certain to happen occasionally when the number of total events is massive. There are two types of low-probability events that are of concern to the engineer: improbable failures, and improbable uses.

When products are used at scale, the improbable becomes probable.

An **improbable failure** happens when something that is very unlikely to fail, fails. For example, a bit in a computer's DRAM might have a one in a billion chance of being flipped by cosmic radiation, per day, but when you have billions of bits of memory, as you do in modern computers, memory corruption is common and occurs on a *daily* basis. [1] If you are producing millions of nails, it's improbable any single nail will have structural issues, but given the sheer number of nails, it is likely that some will.

Improbable uses are usages of products in ways not envisioned by the designer of the product. When there are so many people using your

---

[1]There are conflicting studies regarding the frequency of bit flips, ranging from hourly to every few days. For a modern study see "DRAM Errors in the Wild: A Large-Scale Field Study" Schroeder et al.

product, you are guaranteed that some of those people will be using it in ways you never imagined. This happens all the time in software. APIs are so commonly used in ways not intended that there is a name for this phenomenon: **Hyrum's law**. Hyrum's law states that "with a sufficient number of users of an API, it does not matter what you promise in the contract: all observable behaviors of your system will be depended on by somebody." [29]

XKCD aptly demonstrates this inevitability in Figure 3.2.

Figure 3.2: XKCD Workflow #1172

There is a great tweet from @effinbirds.com in Figure 3.3, which is a real-world example of Hyrum's law and improbable uses.

As an engineer, you should attempt to predict the ways your products could be misused and build preventative measures into the products. In the physical world, children will sometimes use bookcases as ladders, leading to the bookcases falling and crushing them. Some bookcase sellers now include wall mounts on their bookcases to prevent this failure mode. You should be like the bookcase sellers and include the software equivalent of wall mounts. In software, there are two ways to prevent misuse. You can either constrain or generalize your product. Constraints are barriers to misuse such as type checking, asserts, rate limiting, and authentication. Generalization means making your code more general so

I was astonished to meet more
than ten people who believed the
Trash on a Mac was a perfectly
normal place to store important
files and had entire filing systems
in there. (I met them generally
because they were mad that they
had accidentally emptied the
trash and that the trash was not
backed up.)

Jul 7, 2023 at 6:45 PM

Figure 3.3: On the multiple usages of the trash bin.

that its intended use cases are expanded to include the potential misuses, thus transforming the misuses into correct uses.

A phenomenon I have seen often is engineers using a utility function to process a type of data that the function was not intended to process, but it just coincidentally happens to work. This is brittle, and is likely to break on the next version of that utility function. As an engineer, it's important to keep this in mind when you are using other people's products. Don't use things in ways they are not intended to be used. This applies to software as well as hardware. Misuse will cause more problems than it's worth.

3.5   Second-Order Effects

Actions often have direct effects which are predictable and straightforward; these effects are called first-order effects. **Second-order effects** occur as a result of the first-order effects. Action A causes B to occur, and B causes C to occur. C is a second-order effect. Let's demonstrate second-order effects with a story.

In many cities, well-meaning politicians vote to enact rent controls in order to lower the cost of housing for the city's residents. These politicians often fail to consider the second-order effects of their legislation. Once rents are stabilized (first-order effect), investors are less likely to build new housing, as it is no longer profitable (second-order). After all, why would an investor spend millions of dollars to build a new housing complex when they are unable to charge the rent required to pay the mortgage? As such, housing supply does not increase, and the shortage of housing increases. The housing situation inevitably gets worse and worse. Ireland enacted housing policies similar to the ones just described, which led to a housing crisis so severe that at one point there were only 716 [13] houses available for rent in the *entire* country!

In fact, when any good's price is fixed, and the price is below the price which would have been set by the laws of supply and demand, then shortages are bound to occur.

In software engineering, I have seen many cases of second-order effects harming products and teams. When continuous integration pipelines become slow and buggy, engineers pack more code into each commit and merge request, slowing down the release of each new feature and mucking up the repository history. When code becomes complex, productivity decreases, which causes team morale to drop and productivity to further decrease.

The second-order effects of products that are used at scale can change the fabric of society. Trains, the printing press, the internet, social media, and phones all have had second-order effects, which are too numerous to list. Ubiquitous products like these affect everything in unpredictable ways.

An engineering choice early in the project can force the engineer's hand into other engineering choices later. This is probably the most common second-order effect we must consider as engineers. If an engineer decided to use a certain database for a project, it sets in motion a whole cascade of effects. This decision puts constraints on the packages that are needed to communicate with the database, the type of servers needed, the ability to scale the project, the cost of scaling the project, the types of engineers that need to be hired for the project, and the list goes on and on.

3.6   Effect of Code Complexity on Productivity

It is misunderstood how much productivity is affected by the complexity of a code base. When complexity is low, engineers can move fast and accomplish much. When complexity is high, productivity grinds to a near halt. It is common knowledge that startups can innovate and ship much faster than big companies. One of the reasons why startups can innovate faster is because the complexity of the code, the bureaucracy, and the office politics is low enough that it is easily manageable by the average engineer.

Complexity leads to difficulty in making changes to a code base. Touching one part of a complex code base often breaks another part. Re-organizing the code or changing the code's abstractions becomes a nightmarish task, and instead of replacing the abstractions to better model the problem, engineers hack together solutions with the existing abstractions. Of course, this just exacerbates the problem and adds to the overall complexity, pushing the hot potato down the line to the next engineer. Eventually, the whole thing will need to be rewritten.

Here is a great story from an ex-Oracle engineer which demonstrates the effects of bad code on productivity [16]

> Oracle Database 12.2.
>
> It is close to 25 million lines of C code.
>
> What an unimaginable horror! You can't change a single line of code in the product without breaking 1000s of existing tests. Generations of programmers have worked on that code under difficult deadlines and filled the code with all kinds of crap.
>
> Very complex pieces of logic, memory management, context switching, etc. are all held together with thousands of flags. The whole code is ridden with mysterious macros that one cannot decipher without picking a notebook and expanding relevant parts of the macros by hand. It can take a day to two days to really understand what a macro does.

Sometimes one needs to understand the values and the effects of 20 different flags to predict how the code would behave in different situations. Sometimes 100s too! I am not exaggerating.

The only reason why this product is still surviving and still works is due to literally millions of tests!

Here is how the life of an Oracle Database developer is:

1. Start working on a new bug.

2. Spend two weeks trying to understand the 20 different flags that interact in mysterious ways to cause this bag.

3. Add one more flag to handle the new special scenario. Add a few more lines of code that checks this flag and works around the problematic situation and avoids the bug.

4. Submit the changes to a test farm consisting of about 100 to 200 servers that would compile the code, build a new Oracle DB, and run the millions of tests in a distributed fashion.

5. Go home. Come the next day and work on something else. The tests can take 20 hours to 30 hours to complete.

6. Go home. Come the next day and check your farm test results. On a good day, there would be about 100 failing tests. On a bad day, there would be about 1000 failing tests. Pick some of these tests randomly and try to understand what went wrong with your assumptions. Maybe there are some 10 more flags to consider to truly understand the nature of the bug.

7. Add a few more flags in an attempt to fix the issue. Submit the changes again for testing. Wait another 20 to 30 hours.

8. Rinse and repeat for another two weeks until you get the mysterious incantation of the combination of flags right.

9. Finally one fine day you would succeed with 0 tests failing.

10. Add a hundred more tests for your new change to ensure that the next developer who has the misfortune of touching this new piece of code never ends up breaking your fix.

11. Submit the work for one final round of testing. Then submit it for review. The review itself may take another 2 weeks to 2 months. So now move on to the next bug to work on.

12. After 2 weeks to 2 months, when everything is complete, the code would be finally merged into the main branch.

The above is a non-exaggerated description of the life of a programmer in Oracle fixing a bug. Now imagine what horror it is going to be to develop a new feature. It takes 6 months to a year (sometimes two years!) to develop a single small feature (say something like adding a new mode of authentication like support for AD authentication).

The fact that this product even works is nothing short of a miracle!

The situation at Oracle is an extreme case of complexity affecting productivity. The code base is so complex that engineers have no hope of predicting the effects of their changes. It's important to note that the reason engineers struggle in this situation is due to their memory not being sufficient to keep track of all the components, variables, and factors on which their change is dependent. The problem is not the complexity, the problem is that our minds can't handle the complexity.

3.7 Broken Windows Theory

The **broken windows theory** is a well-known theory in criminology that attempts to explain criminal and anti-social behavior in neighborhoods. The theory states that

> "that visible signs of crime, anti-social behavior and civil disorder create an urban environment that encourages further crime and disorder, including serious crimes. The theory suggests that policing methods that target minor crimes such as vandalism, loitering, public drinking, jaywalking, and fare evasion help to create an atmosphere of order and lawfulness."
> [22]

The theory is named after the example stated by the authors, "one unrepaired broken window is a signal that no one cares, and so breaking more windows costs nothing. (It has always been fun.)"[27]

One broken window starts a chain reaction leading to more broken windows. This is a very bad chain reaction to start. It's like leaving a bit of rust on a metal object. Once the rust takes hold, it spreads very fast. But if the rust is prevented from taking hold in the first place, the spread will not occur.

The broken windows effect occurs in software just as much as it does in neglected neighborhoods. Low-quality code leads engineers to write more low-quality code. Nobody wants to be that guy who stands out with the lowest quality code in a code base. But if everyone is writing bad code, then it excuses any individual to do the same. The powerful social incentives which discourage bad behavior are lost when everyone is behaving badly. Thus, a small bit of bad code should not be seen as an isolated problem. It should be seen as a broken window, as a catalyst for systemic rot.

Beyond the broken windows effect, bad code causes harm by leading to a loss of team morale. Working and trying to make changes in a messy code base is frustrating and emotionally draining. Talent leaves the company, and good engineers stay away.

3.8   Stories

3.8.1   The Laptop Bios

A few months ago, I visited my brother and his family. As usual, whenever I visit family members, the question arises. "Zohar, can you help me fix. . . ?" This time, my brother's laptop needed fixing. When I powered it on, it would start loading the bios and then abruptly restart. The laptop was stuck in this loop. My brother had Googled the problem and called the company's support line. He followed the instructions to reset the bios, a combination of pressing and holding keys, but to no avail. He was ready to send the laptop in for repair, as it was still under warranty.

I started with Google as my brother had, tried a number of other things, and followed the "bios reset" instructions I found on the manufacturer's website, but nothing worked. The laptop was still stuck in an endless loop. I kept on Googling, and eventually, on some hidden page, tucked behind a few corners of the internet, I chanced upon an alternative "bios reset" sequence. I tried this different sequence and sure enough, the laptop came back to life.

So what happened? The engineers who designed this particular model decided, for one reason or another, to use a bios reset sequence that was different from the standard sequence the manufacturer used. This particular model's sequence did not make it to the company's troubleshooting website and did not make it to the tech support representative who tried to help my brother.

I wonder how many other customers faced the same situation as my brother? How many customers returned their laptops? How much did the non-standard choice of bios reset sequence end up costing the company? How many customers decided not to buy another model from this company?

Did the engineers who chose this alternative bios reset sequence imagine how much it would cost the company? Probably not. It is hard to imagine these things. But that does not mean that this was unavoidable. If the engineers had followed design principles such as constancy, following the path, and communicating with the user, this whole situation could have been avoided. We will discuss these principles in the next chapter.

3.8.2 Virality

Starting a social media app is a hard **chicken-and-egg problem**. For users to be interested in using the app, it must already have people using it. Getting those first users is a challenging problem, though, because they are not incentivized by an existing user base.

One way of solving this problem is through viral growth. Users are given the ability to invite their friends, with the hopes of creating a **viral effect**. Virality occurs when, on average, each new user successfully brings to the platform more than one user, thus creating a reinforcing chain reaction, until everyone is using the app. **R-value** is a term that signifies the average number of new users each user brings. Thus, an r-value greater than 1 leads to the product growing virally, and an r-value less than 1 leads to the app falling out of use. The success of a social app is often dependent on its r-value. A high r-value will guarantee initial success.

Many UI/UX studies have shown that user sign-up rates are dependent on the number of steps the user must take to sign up. For every extra field the user must fill out, the sign-up rate drops by a few percent.

Now consider how the success of a social app can be dependent on the number of steps needed to join. Too many steps, and an otherwise viral app will drop below an r-value of 1 and fail to spread. The difference can come down to just one step too many—one step too many, and the product fails. Consider that a team of engineers, designers, PMs, an entire company's success can depend on just one single step being removed from a sign-up process.

3.8.3 NHS Mapping Error

In 2016, a bug in the UK National Health Service (NHS) medical records systems was discovered, which led to the 10-year cardiovascular risk score, or QRISK2 score, of patients being miscalculated. These scores were used by doctors to determine medication and treatment plans for the patients. It is estimated that over 300,000 patients were affected by this error. Upon discovery of the bug, the NHS wrote a letter to clinicians that stated:

> The issue occurred when the QRISK2 calculator on SystmOne was pre-populated with entries from the medical record, or when QRISK2 scores were used to identify patients through Clinical Reporting.
>
> ...
>
> The main clinical risk for patients arises when the change in score has taken them above or below the threshold at which treatment is usually considered. [5]

It sounds like the technical issue was relatively minor; they write that it was due to a "mapping error." It probably took an engineer a few minutes to fix. But let's consider the damage it caused. Thousands of patients received medication that they should not have, and thousands did not receive medication that they should have. Some patients suffered from anxiety about receiving a bad score, and some erroneously decided to eat less healthily because they believed their hearts were healthy and at a low risk for a cardiovascular event. Some patients most likely suffered heart attacks that they otherwise would not have had if they had received the proper treatment!

Notice the outsized effects a simple mapping error can have, due to the scale and importance of the product. I am not familiar with the code behind the error, but if I had to, I would bet that the error occurred due to the code being overly complex. This was most likely a case of harm caused by complexity. Notice the non-continuous nature of the effects of the bug. Patients only received medication if the QRISK2 score was above a certain threshold. The quantity of medication was not given in proportion to their score, but rather in an all-or-nothing fashion.

3.9   Urinals

Let's sidetrack for a moment and discuss urinals. I apologize for the crudeness of the topic, but I could not pass on the opportunity—urinals are a great example of poor design, second-order effects, and the effects of scale. Urinals are probably the worst-designed widely used products. I could write an entire book just about urinals, but I will spare you that pleasure.

Figure 3.4: Classic North American urinal

If you go into any restroom with a urinal, you will notice somewhere between a few drops to a pool of urine on the floor below the urinal. At busy restrooms, such as those at airports, malls, or bars, you are almost guaranteed a pool of urine. These pools smell bad, track on the bottom of our shoes, and spread throughout the restroom and into the nearby spaces. The pools are not the only thing wrong with urinals, they are simply the most visible. Splash-back onto the user's pants and the unhygienic nature of the flush handle are two other first-order problems with urinals.

Let's start with the pools of urine. There are two primary causes for these pools. The first is caused by the gap between the user and the urinal lip. Urine inevitably falls in that gap. The second cause is due to splash-back, i.e. the reflection of urine bouncing off the urinal and onto the floor. Splash-back not only gets urine on the floor but also on to the user's pants.

In high-traffic areas, the urine accumulates so rapidly that janitors are hired to constantly be cleaning the restrooms. At airports, janitors are assigned a few restrooms and spend the day traveling between them wiping up the urine pools.

Let's look at the problem from a design perspective. How much harm is caused by the poor design of urinals?

The first-order effects of the design are the pools of urine and the splash-back onto users' pants, both of which reduce the pleasantness of the restroom experience.

The second-order effects are numerous. There are the costs of hiring janitors to clean the urine and the extra loads of laundry that users will need to keep their pants from smelling. More loads of washing means more pollution in our rivers, higher energy demand, and pants wearing out much faster. More janitors mean airports have higher expenses and higher airfare prices. The wet floors probably occasionally cause users to slip and fall. Urine and urea are tracked on shoes and end up on the carpets outside of the restroom, leading to discoloration and degradation. Nothing catastrophic, but pretty bad considering this can all be easily avoided.

3.9.1   The Incentives Are Wrong

Consider what the designer of a urinal is asking the user to do. The users are being asked to step in piss, press a dirty handle, and succumb to splash-back. Why would anybody agree to this? There is no incentive for them to do it, and that is the first problem with urinal design.

Users have a **perverse incentive.**A perverse incentive is one that rewards the wrong behavior. Users have an incentive to stand as far back as possible. The further back the user stands the less urine gets on his shoes, and the less splash-back onto his pants. As the pool of urine grows in size, users stand further and further back. Of course, the further back one stands the more urine ends in the pool on the floor. This leads to a destructive feedback loop of the pool growing, users standing back and the pool growing faster. Incentives are the primary driver of behavior, as Charlie Munger, the great investor and hobbyist psychologist writes: "If you want to get the right behavior, provide the right incentives." [11]

Another way of looking at this is that the cost of peeing on the floor is external to the user, i.e. the user does not **internalize** the cost of their misuse. The way to avoid **tragedy of commons** situations like these is to **internalize externalities**, thus aligning incentives. In this case, you would want to design the urinal in such a way that standing further back led to more splash-back on the user's pants.

The same perverse incentive problems hold for the flushing mechanism. Users have no incentive to touch a dirty, genital-bacteria-infested handle, and so they often don't. This leads to urine building up in the bottom of the urinal leading to more and grosser splash-back (as it's someone else's urine being splashed back).

If the designers of the urinals would have thought about the problem more deeply and used the design principles taught in this book, the world would be a better place. In the case studies section in Book II of this series, we will come back to urinals and show how they should be designed.

3.10 There Is Hope

In short, it is impossible to accurately predict all of the effects and potential harm of a given design choice. We cannot think of all the ways our design can go wrong, and defend against every one. Instead, we must design in a way that generically reduces the ways things can go wrong. For instance, if we know that parts have a tendency to break (but don't know exactly which ones will break or what will cause them to break), we can design systems with fewer parts, thus reducing the likelihood of the overall system failing. If we know humans are likely to make mistakes, we should reduce the complexity of our designs to reduce the likelihood of mistakes.

Jackson's law is not intended to make us despair at the impossibility of creating harmless, perfect products. The law should not be interpreted to imply that engineers should labor until their products are perfect. Rather, the purpose is to teach the limitations of our cognition and the importance of designing carefully and following best practices. Being careful in your work is critical to creating great products. You must think carefully about what you are creating, how it can go wrong, how it can go right, how it can lead to harm, and what can be done to reduce the probability and magnitude of the harm. And you must realize the limitations of your careful thinking and follow best practices to counteract those limitations.

Chapter 4

Design and Engineering for Humans

Design adds value faster than it adds costs
— Joel Spolsky[1], Founder of Stack Overflow and Trello

4.1 Coding Is a Design Problem

People often think of design as relating to the parts of a product that end-users interact with, typically the user interface (UI) and the user experience (UX). Engineering typically refers to how the product works, the mechanics, and what is going on behind the scenes. As engineers, we must not forget that design also refers to the design of the engineering. This means that it must be designed not only for the end-user but for the engineers working on the project. The engineering, everything from the high-level abstractions to the variable names, must be understandable, modifiable, and maintainable by engineers.

In this book, our discussions of design primarily concern the design of the engineering. Despite this, most of the ideas presented apply to all types of design, including UI/UX. The ideas are mostly universal in that design is about navigating the needs, idiosyncrasies, and capabilities of all humans.

Writing code is more of a design problem than an engineering problem.

---

[1]One Friday night in Jerusalem, I found myself at my friend's parent's house for a family dinner. I struck up a conversation with the quiet, elderly woman sitting next to me. I mentioned that I work in software, and she in turn told me that her son does too! I asked what type of software and she told me he made a website which he now runs. "Cool!" I responded, "what's his website?" "Stack Overflow, have you heard of it?".

The engineering is usually straightforward, whereas the design is typically difficult.

4.1.1 Aspects of Good Design

We have discussed how reducing complexity is key to good design. When complexity is reduced, good design will usually magically appear. Thus, reducing complexity often has positive side effects not directly related to cognitive complexity. These positive side effects that emerge happen to be the fundamental aspects of good design. Let's review them briefly.

1. Functionality and usability: A good design should serve its intended purpose effectively and efficiently. It should be easy to use and should work as intended.

2. Aesthetics: A good design should be visually appealing and should consider the overall look and feel of the product, system, or experience.

3. User-friendliness: A good design should be easy to understand and use, and should consider the needs and preferences of the user.

4. Flexibility: A good design should be adaptable and able to evolve over time to meet changing needs and preferences.

5. Accessibility: A good design should be inclusive and consider the needs of people with limited knowledge and memories, or non-native English speakers.

6. Durability: A good design should be durable against wear and tear, a changing environment, and user error.

This list is mostly obvious, but it is still useful to state it explicitly and keep it in mind when designing. What is not obvious is how to achieve good designs.

4.1.2 GNU Tar

On *nix systems such as Unix, Linux, and MacOS, the GNU tar program is the most widely used tool for archiving and unarchiving files. If you have used the tar program, then you are probably well aware of how annoying it is to use. In fact, it's so bad that XKCD has a comic about it.

Figure 4.1: XKCD Tar #1168

Today the most frequent use of tar is to extract a gzipped tar archive. The command to do this is as follows:

```
$ tar -xzf documents.tar.gz
```

Where the arguments are as follows:

```
x - Extract to disk from the archive.
z - Decompress the files. i.e. unzip
f - the file to operate on
```

As XKCD aptly conveys, the command is hard to remember and often forgotten. Making matters worse, the tar man pages [2] do not contain an example explaining how to use the command for the most frequently used case. And trying to figure out the correct arguments from the dense documentation is a tedious and difficult task. As XKCD again points out in Figure 4.2, you should not need to read the documentation to use a toaster. Tools, especially simple ones, should be usable with minimal, or ideally zero, reading of documentation.

---

[2] Man pages are the go-to documentation for GNU programs such as tar.

Figure 4.2: XKCD RTFM #293

Over my many years of using *nix systems, I have probably spent a few hours of my life searching for the correct tar arguments. Every time I need to use tar I get frustrated. Assuming my experience is common amongst tar users, if we multiply the number of tar users by the average amount of time and frustration they each have spent, we arrive at a very large number. The amount of harm caused by the bad design of tar is ridiculous.

What design principles should have been applied when designing tar to ensure this harm did not occur in the first place? The main principle that was lacking in application here is the principle of **maximizing user convenience**. The principle is self-explanatory; products should be made to be maximally convenient for their users. The product may be a command-line interface, an API, a user interface, a function, or even a code base.

The best way to maximize convenience is to focus on the most common use cases of the product. In the case of tar, that would be extracting and decompressing archives. The lowest-hanging fruit, the first thing to do, is to update the man pages with an example of the most common use case. This can be done today and will not cause backward-compatibility issues or break anyone's scripts. Documentation should *always* include examples of the most frequent use cases. It's cheap to do and the benefit is immense.

Both tar's documentation and interface can be improved. A much better interface would be one in which no arguments are needed for the most common use case. If I were designing it, I would split the interface into two, so that there would be a tar and untar command. The untar command would be used as follows:

```
$ untar documents.tar.gz
```

In fact, dividing the program into two commands and using default arguments that work in the most common use cases is how GNU zip is designed, which consists of the zip and unzip commands. You should note that there are no XKCD comics complaining about zip.

4.1.3 Automation

In my recommended redesign of tar, the program will automatically detect that the passed file is compressed and extract it using the correct compression algorithm. **Automation** is a great technique that should be used wherever possible to increase convenience. Previously, we discussed how automation in the case of an automatic transmission reduces the cognitive load on drivers by hiding complexity, but it also has the benefit of increasing convenience. Automation reduces the effort required from users to accomplish their objectives. Automation also reduces the likelihood of user error; a user can't make an error if the responsibility lies with the machine. Finally, automation enables the designer to hide the implementation from the user, enabling the designer to optimize the implementation at a later date without requiring the user to learn something new, change their code, or be negatively affected.

Another approach to improving the tar interface is to keep a single interface but add automation with sane defaults. For example, the program could detect if the passed file is already compressed and archived, and if so, unarchive and decompress it without needing the user to specify their desires.

It is easy to criticize and find fault in a design. It is harder to step back and give the designers **the benefit of the doubt**. As humans, we should resist **attribution bias**, which is the tendency to explain a person's actions through their character or skills, rather than environmental circumstances. We are biased to over-weight a person's personality and under-weight the situational factors. For example, if someone says something that you think is mean, instead of attributing it to them being a mean person, you should consider that maybe they had a bad day, or maybe you misinterpreted what they said. In engineering, we are often quick to judge another engineer's code and design choices without understanding the full context in which they were made. Maybe there were good reasons that an ugly hack was needed or that the tar interface is inconvenient.

The tar command was built a long, long time ago in computer history; computers were very different back then, and the needs of users have changed significantly. Maybe the design choices made for tar were optimal at the time of its design but are not ideal for how we use tar today. After all, tar archives were originally used to store files on magnetic tapes (the default storage medium before hard drives). In fact, the name "tar" itself stands for "tape archiver." Maybe the maintainers of tar were unable to improve the design without breaking backward compatibility. Using tar to untar compressed files from the internet was definitely not the most common use case, as it is today; in fact, the internet did not even exist.

4.1.4   Bad Design Is Forever

Bad design is forever is the idea that certain designs last much longer than one would expect. When the creators of tar wrote the code in 1979, I doubt they thought tar would still be used 40+ years later. Who thought a utility for tape archives would still be widely used in the age of quantum computers? Again, we see that the future is hard to predict.

A good example of "bad design is forever" is a story from the early days of computing written by Rob Landley.

You know how Ken Thompson and Dennis Ritchie created Unix on a PDP-7 in 1969? Well around 1971 they upgraded to a PDP-11 with a pair of RK05 disk packs (1.5 megabytes each) for storage.

When the operating system grew too big to fit on the first RK05 disk pack (their root filesystem) they let it leak into the second one, which is where all the user home directories lived (which is why the mount was called /usr). They replicated all the OS directories under there (/bin, /sbin, /lib, /tmp...) and wrote files to those new directories because their original disk was out of space. When they got a third disk, they mounted it on /home and relocated all the user directories to there so the OS could consume all the space on both disks and grow to THREE WHOLE MEGABYTES (ooooh!).

Of course they made rules about "when the system first boots, it has to come up enough to be able to mount the second disk on /usr, so don't put things like the mount command /usr/bin or we'll have a chicken and egg problem bringing the system up. " Fairly straightforward. Also fairly specific to v6 unix of 35 years ago.

The /bin vs /usr/bin split (and all the others) is an artifact of this, a 1970's implementation detail that got carried forward for decades by bureaucrats who never question *why* they're doing things. It stopped making any sense before Linux was ever invented, for multiple reasons... [9]

To add to the mess, it turns out /usr doesn't stand for "user" but for "user system resources." I remember getting confused by this directory name in my early days of using Linux. I would look for my personal files in the /usr/ directory instead of the /home/ directory. I imagine many other engineers also experience similar confusion.

The *nix directory structure is an extreme example of bad design surviving almost forever. Most bad design is not actually forever, but some designs have a tendency to be more sticky than others. In Chapter 5, we discuss how data schemas, interfaces, abstractions, names, protocols, and formats tend to have long lifespans and that more care should be taken when designing them.

4.2   Human Error Is Design Error

My inability to remember the tar command arguments, or being confused by the Linux directory structure, should not be blamed on my poor memory or on my ignorance, but rather on poor design.

In the book *The Design of Everyday Things* Don Norman writes that "**human error is design error.**" [15]. We will review his ideas in this section [3]. Norman writes

> Most industrial accidents are caused by human error: esti-
> mates range between 75 and 95 percent. How is it that so
> many people are so incompetent? Answer: They aren't. It's a
> design problem. ... Human error usually is a result of poor de-
> sign: it should be called system error. Humans err continually;
> it is an intrinsic part of our nature. System design should take
> this into account. Pinning the blame on the person may be
> a comfortable way to proceed, but why was the system ever
> designed so that a single act by a single person could cause
> calamity? Worse, blaming the person without fixing the root,
> underlying cause does not fix the problem: the same error is
> likely to be repeated by someone else. [15]

When something goes wrong and a human did something which directly caused the thing to go wrong, we have a tendency to immediately blame the human. For example, if there is a car accident, the first person we usually blame is the driver. Blaming the driver is easy; the driver is immediately in front of us (availability bias) and after all, they are the ones who failed to press the brakes in time. But a slightly deeper analysis might reveal that the street was not properly lit, the speed limit was set too high, or the driver education system is insufficient. Blaming the driver

---

[3]For a better and more thorough review of his great ideas, you should read *The Design of Everyday Thing (New York: Basic Books, 2013)*

will not solve other drivers from making the same error; it will not do any good, or make the world a better place. In order to prevent the error from re-occurring, we must understand and fix the **underlying cause**.

In software engineering, we often blame the user, our fellow engineers, or even ourselves. We might think that the user does not know how to use the software, or failed to properly read the documentation. Maybe the user is an idiot and doesn't understand how to implement safe memory management in C++. Is it a coincidence that nearly everyone, even the most experienced engineers, make errors and write unsafe C++ code? No, it is not, it is due to the poor design of the language. The same engineers don't write code with memory bugs when writing code in Rust, a language designed to be memory safe.

The same logic holds true for your own errors. If you are having a hard time understanding some code, it's probably not your fault, but the fault of the code. We could be quick and blame the author of the code, but maybe it's not their fault either. Maybe the system they are part of (the organization or team) is designed in such a way, or has incentive structures, that force the writing of bad code. A good technique for discovering who is really to blame is called the "**five whys**". The technique of the five whys was originally developed by Sakichi Toyoda at Toyota.

4.2.1 Five Whys

The "five whys" is a problem-solving technique that involves asking why a problem occurred repeatedly until the root cause of the problem is identified. It is based on the idea that most problems can be traced back to their root cause by asking "why" about five times.

Here is an example of how the technique might be used to solve a problem:

Number	Question	Answer
1	Why did the production website go down?	Because someone made changes to production instead of staging.
2	Why did they make changes to production instead of staging?	Because they thought they were actually making changes to staging.
3	Why did they think they were working with staging?	Because they were confused. It was human error.
4	Why were they confused?	Because the domain of production is only one character different than the domain of staging.
5	Why are the domains names only one character different?	Because the system was not designed defensively against human error.

In this scenario, we were able to find what needed to be changed to prevent this specific error after only four whys. The five in five whys is just an average; sometimes more are required, sometimes less.

In the above example, most people will stop at question 3. Human error caused the problem, let's move on. But blaming the problem on human error is not going to prevent it from happening again. In this case, renaming the two environments so that they are less similar would reduce the likelihood of engineers making this mistake in the future. Or one can be more cautious and require the deployer of changes to type out "production" or "staging" to initiate the deployment.

Don Norman writes:

> Designers should strive to minimize the chance of inappropriate actions in the first place ... If a person performs an inappropriate action, the design should maximize the chance that this can be discovered and then rectified. This requires good, intelligible feedback coupled with a simple, clear conceptual model. [15]

One last thing to be said is that when designing for human error, you should assume **Murphy's law**. Murphy's law states that "Anything that can go wrong will go wrong." Every possible mistake a person can make will be made. The user might be distracted, rushed, tired, inexperienced, or press the wrong key. Sometimes they will misinterpret a name of a variable. A friend of mine has a story where he misunderstood a variable name, and ended up writing code that accidentally refunded hundreds of customers. It ended up costing his employer $40,000. Whoever named that variable, would never have thought that it would or even could lead to a $40,000 loss for his employer. There are so many ways things can go wrong, it's impossible to imagine all of them. And because of that, it is critical to write code and design systems such that the space of possible things going wrong is constrained. One of your jobs as a designer is to prevent known errors, and constrain the unknown.

Keep in mind the existence of **optimism bias**, the bias of assuming positive outcomes and that things won't go wrong. Murphy's law is a great mental tool for counteracting optimism bias.

4.3 Design Requires Thinking

The first step in designing is thinking. Before you start designing or writing any code, you must take a step back and think carefully. You must think about your users, the future usages, how requirements will change, how the product will evolve, how things can go wrong, how things can go right, what is known, and what is unknown. You must consider the high-level architecture and the low-level details. There is a lot to think about. In fact, there is too much to think about. It is impossible to consider all the possibilities and think about all that must be taken into account just by trying hard. This is why engineers and designers have developed best practices, design patterns, design rules, and other various tools. These tools enable us to arrive at good designs without needing to think about **everything**. They are time-tested maps to direct us in the optimization search space.

4.3.1 Consider the Bigger Picture. Consider the System.

Richard Hamming wrote in his book *The Art of Doing Science and Engineering* (Stripe Press, 2020) that "Systems engineering is the attempt to keep at all times the larger goals in mind and to translate local actions into global results." [7]. Hamming provides the following parable.

A man was examining the construction of a cathedral. He

asked a stone mason what he was doing chipping the stones, and the mason replied, "I am making stones". He asked a stone carver what he was doing, "I am carving a gargoyle". And so it went, each person said in detail what they were doing. Finally he came to an old woman who was sweeping the ground. She said, "I am helping build a cathedral". [7]

If your code is part of a larger code base or project, then it is part of a system. Even if your code is a standalone script, if it will be used by humans (yourself or others), it is part of a system. Anything that consists of elements interacting is a system. Systems are everywhere once you open your eyes.

As Hamming's story demonstrates, we are biased to be blind to the bigger picture and often get stuck in the details. The biggest picture to consider is your objective, as we have discussed previously. Losing track of your objectives will lead to much wasted energy and time.

A phenomenon I often see is as follows. A user requests a new feature from an engineer. The engineer does not stop and consider why the user is requesting this feature and how the feature is intended to be used. The engineer does not consider the bigger picture. The engineer simply soldiers forward and builds the feature. Often, it turns out that the feature requested is not the optimal way of achieving the user's goal. Or maybe the desired functionality already existed in a part of the system that the user was unfamiliar with. Soldiering forward without understanding the bigger picture usually leads to unnecessary work occurring and the feature needing to be modified or removed at a later date.

As an example, consider a user who requests a button to export some data as a CSV file. The user does not state his reason to the engineer and the engineer does not ask. Let's say the reason behind the user's request is that they want to be able to visualize the data in a different tool. Maybe the best thing to do in this case is to embed the visualization directly in the system and reduce all the manual work that will be needed to export and import data between the tools. Or maybe the visualization tool has an API, and the data can be moved in a more automated way.

The way to prevent this unfortunate situation is to ask lots of questions and understand the reasons behind requests. It is amazing how much value I have added just by asking questions, discovering things that don't make sense, and then fixing them.

4.3.2 The User Is Drunk

The user is drunk is a design concept by Richard Littauer. The central idea is that you should design your UI/UX so straightforwardly that even a drunk user could use it. A drunk user needs a simple interface, a distraction-free interface, an interface that does not require thinking. Thinking while drunk is likely to lead to errors, and thus should not be required. You should design a system that has protections against user errors so that the wrong user action does not lead to catastrophe.

This concept is helpful for getting you into the correct mindset and lowering your expectations of your users. Most likely, your users are not drunk, but they are probably distracted, rushed, or tired, which is not so dissimilar from being drunk.

4.3.3 Enter Your User's Shoes

Steve Jobs said: "You have to start with the customer experience and work your way back to technology." In Chapter 2, we discussed that in order to write lowest reasonable denominator code, one should build a model of their LRD users' knowledge and skills. In addition to their knowledge and skill, you must also consider their objectives and how they will interact with your product. Charles Eames, a world-renowned designer, once said: "The role of the designer is that of a good, thoughtful host anticipating the needs of his guests." If you can't anticipate your user's needs, how can you build products that are useful for them? Below are questions that you should consider when designing that will help you anticipate your user's needs.

- What are the most common ways the user interacts with the product? How can the product be improved to optimize the most common interactions?

- What interfaces, features, and automations can be implemented that will improve the user experience?

- What are the objectives and priorities of the user?

- What are the user's pain points and challenges?

- What are the user's expectations and preferences?

- What does the LRD user know and what do they not know?

Correctly answering these questions is impossible. You cannot know all of your users' needs and objectives; you are likely to make false assumptions and poor inferences given your limited knowledge. And even if you could know your users' needs, they are likely to change over time.

That being said, as you develop a habit of asking these questions, you will learn through retrospection and user feedback where you erred in your answers to the above questions. You will improve at entering the shoes of your users and, thus, improve your design skills.

In some cases, it is possible to directly ask your users these questions. If you find yourself having low confidence in your answers to these questions, getting feedback from your users provides a very high return on investment. Besides asking users questions directly, you can sit with them and observe how they interact with your product and code. Observe where they get confused and what interaction errors they make. And of course, you should blame errors on the design, not on the user.

Asking and observing your users, unfortunately, is not enough to ensure your design is aligned with their objectives. The user's objectives are likely to change, your objectives are likely to change, and the technology is likely to change—in fact, everything is likely to change. This is why an engineer must prepare for the future.

4.3.4   Design for the Futures

Predicting and planning for the future is very hard, since there is so much uncertainty in the world. An old Yiddish proverb describes the situation well: "Man plans; God laughs." [4]

I use the term futures and not future because there are many possible futures, and all of them should be considered when designing. Each future has a certain probability of occurring, and that probability must also be taken into account. In the next chapter, we introduce this idea more formally and relate the futures to a measurement of cost. We call this relationship a **probabilistic cost distribution over time** and will explain it in detail later on. But for now, let's keep it simple.

The first (and probably most effective) technique for planning for the future is to follow basic design and engineering principles such as simplicity, minimalism, redundancy, and reducing cognitive load. Code that follows these principles will be much easier to smith into whatever is needed in the future. The great thing about these principles is that you don't even need to predict what the future may hold to benefit.

The next technique requires thinking. You must think about what the future will look like and how it will affect your product. You must consider the probabilities of each future and calculate the for each one, the cost–benefit ratios of all the possible design choices. It takes experience to get good at this. With years of engineering experience and actively paying attention to when things go wrong, you will get better. Here are some questions to prime your thinking:

- In what ways may users (end-users and engineers) intentionally or unintentionally misuse this product/code?

- How may the requirements change?

- Will this need to scale? If so, how much?

- What usage errors are users likely to make when using the product?

- What additions to the software are likely to be needed in the future?

- In which directions will the code rot over time? What changes can be made today to reduce future code rot?

---

[4] "The Yiddish rhymes and is more catchy: Der mentsh trakht un got lakht"

- What future changes to the code are likely to break the current code? Is the code barely running or is it robust to changes?

- How will hardware and computing trends affect the product?

- What future regulations may affect the product?

- What are the worst-case scenarios?

Considering these questions and taking **defensive precautions** to minimize possible negative futures is a key to good engineering. These precautions include asserts, error messages, automated tests, flexibility, and simplicity.

The term **margin of safety** in mechanical engineering refers to the strength of the system above what is needed for an intended load or use. It's essentially a buffer for safety to account for uncertainties or unexpected events. The margin of safety is designed to ensure that even if the system experiences unexpected stresses or if there are inaccuracies in the design models and calculations, it will not fail.

For instance, if a bridge is designed to carry a maximum load of 10,000 kg, the engineers might actually design it to withstand 20,000 kg to add a margin of safety. That extra 10,000 kg is the margin of safety, and it provides a buffer in case the load ever exceeds the expected 10,000 kg, or in the case of unexpected occurrences like structural wear, extreme weather conditions, earthquakes, or some simultaneous combination of these factors.

$$\text{Margin of safety} = \frac{\text{failure load}}{\text{design load}} - 1$$

Figure 4.3: Margin of safety equation

The amount of margin of safety required often depends on the consequences of failure, and the level of uncertainty in the design models. In some critical systems like aircraft, a high margin of safety is crucial because the consequences of failure are likely to be catastrophic. The point here is that you must choose your margin of safety carefully. Too much safety is expensive, and too little is often catastrophic. In Book II, we will introduce techniques of defensive programming and demonstrate how to be more defensive in your code without incurring a large cost.

4.4 Let the System Evolve (Gall's Law)

Gall's law is a principle in systems thinking which states that a complex system that works invariably has evolved from a simple system that worked. This law applies to software development in the sense that complex software systems are often built up from simpler systems that have been tested and proven to work. Remember, nearly all aspects of code should be considered a system; even a few functions interacting with each other is a system.

One way to apply Gall's law in software development is to start with a small, simple system and incrementally build upon it, rather than trying to design a complex system all at once. This approach can help to reduce the risk of failure and make the development process more manageable. Not following Gall's law often leads to over-engineering and systems far more complicated than necessary. Start simple, and only add complexity when you are sure the simple does not work. A great example of this is the Stack Overflow system architecture presented in section 5.9. Notice how a super-capable system like Stack Overflow runs perfectly with a ridiculously simple design. Their engineers started simple and did not need to evolve, or I should say devolve, into the complex.

Another way to apply Gall's law in software development is to focus on building modular, reusable components that can be composed to create more complex systems. By breaking a complex system down into smaller, simpler parts, it can be easier to understand and maintain.

If you try to build a complex system from the ground up without letting it evolve over time, you are almost certain to fail, and if not completely fail, then at least produce a sub-optimal result.

In *Thinking in Systems* by Donella H. Meadows (Chelsea Green Publishing, 2008) is the following parable:

There were once two watchmakers, named Hora and Tempus. Both of them made fine watches, and they both had many customers. People dropped into their stores, and their phones rang constantly with new orders. Over the years, however, Hora prospered, while Tempus became poorer and poorer. That's because Hora discovered the principle of hierarchy...

The watches made by Hora and Tempus consisted of about one thousand parts each. Tempus put his together in such a way that if he had one partly assembled and had to put it down— to answer the phone, say— it fell to pieces. When he came back to it, Tempus would have to start all over again. The more his customers phoned him, the harder it became for him to find enough uninterrupted time to finish a watch.

Hora's watches were no less complex than those of Tempus, but he put together stable subassemblies of about ten elements each. Then he put ten of these subassemblies together into a larger assembly; and ten of those assemblies constituted the whole watch. Whenever Hora had to put down a partly completed watch to answer the phone, he lost only a small part of his work. So he made his watches much faster and more efficiently than did Tempus.

Complex systems can evolve from simple systems only if there are stable intermediate forms. The resulting complex forms will naturally be hierarchic. That may explain why hierarchies are so common in the systems nature presents to us. Among all possible complex forms, hierarchies are the only ones that have had the time to evolve. [10]

4.5   Communicate with the User

One of the big challenges in design is communicating with the user. How is a user supposed to know how to use the product? How are they supposed to know its breaking points and failure modes? How are they supposed to know how what actions to take when the product does not work as expected?

As a software engineer, you experience the challenges of communication whenever you read someone else's code. We are all too familiar with the challenges of reading another person's code; sometimes it's easy, but more often than not it is quite difficult. The creators of Python, aware of the difficulty engineers have in reading code, made readability one of the primary principles in the design of the language (see The Zen of Python in the appendix). **Readability** is the quality of being easy to read and understand. When code is more readable, less cognitive load is induced, fewer bugs are created, and productivity is increased. Code with high readability is also a pleasure to work with, which I believe is one of the reasons that Python has become so popular.

When humans communicate in natural language, we use a set of words with mutually agreed-upon meanings. When someone uses the word "dog," I know more or less what they mean. Despite the set of mutually agreed-upon words, communication *is still difficult*! Humans are constantly misunderstanding each other, and to make matters worse we often don't realize a misunderstanding occurred. And if it does become apparent, it is often only after the fact, when things have already gone wrong.

Since communication is difficult even with a mutually agreed upon set of words, consider how much more difficult it is without agreement on the meanings of words. This occurs, for example, when we attempt to communicate with someone who speaks an unfamiliar language. We can use hand gestures, body language, and facial expressions, but the bandwidth and depth of communication is quite limited.

In software engineering, our set of mutually agreed-upon words is similarly very limited. There are the reserved words and syntax of the programming language itself, but that's about it. Without these reserved words, understanding another person's code would be near impossible. It would be equivalent to reading code in a programming language which you have never studied. This might not sound so bad if you are familiar with the reserved words and syntax. But some languages that use esoteric reserved words and syntax are quite unreadable to the untrained. Just try reading Perl, Lisp, or Haskell and see for yourself!

The functions and classes that we create can be considered custom extensions of the original programming language. Their names can be thought of as the equivalent of reserved words. These names are words that are *not* mutually agreed upon, however. The person on the other end of the communication does not know the meaning of these words. Nevertheless, the writer of the code has decided to use them anyway and communicate in a made-up language.

Good names are so important because they are the primary means of communication between engineers in a made-up language. Names should assume that the person reading them has no idea what the entity they represent is, so as such, they should be descriptive and specific. Descriptive and specific names, of course, come at the cost of length and verbosity, but this is a good tradeoff to make as long as you don't go overboard. As an engineer, when reading another person's code, I prefer the names to be long and descriptive so that I don't have to constantly search through the code trying to figure out what each name signifies.

Furthermore, for names, information should be communicated through the logic of the code. Logic that is simple, that runs in a predictable step-by-step sequence (instead of a convoluted order) helps to decrease cognitive load and communicate information.

Another trick we humans use to communicate and reduce cognitive load is conventions such as styling guides. For example, many style guides suggest one naming convention for variables and a different one for functions. This type of convention enables an engineer to instantly know if a name is a variable or a function. The convention is communicating information. Even natural languages have similar informative conventions, such as English's usage of capitalization to indicate the beginnings of sentences and proper nouns.

Finally, there are the explicit forms of communication such as documentation and comments. These are often critical in software as there is only so much that can be communicated through names and logic.

To be clear, the aim is not just to communicate, but to communicate with a high bandwidth while having a very low miscommunication or error rate. If your user needs to read a manual, it is usually a sign that your design is not great. Low-bandwidth communication (such as through manuals) is easy for the designer, but typically not that useful. Your job as a designer is to mix and match the various tools of communication so that the required information is conveyed to the user with minimal effort on *their* part.

4.5.1   Feedback

Feedback is critical to communication. We are so used to feedback in our inter-human communication that it often does not enter our conscious awareness. When talking to another person, we are constantly giving each other feedback with facial expressions, body posture, proximity, tone of voice, and, of course, words. We are creatures whose minds expect feedback and are inevitably frustrated when we don't receive it.

Computers, as of now, are unable to provide the quality of feedback that we are accustomed to in our interpersonal communication. This lack of quality feedback leads to reduced productivity, frustration, and sometimes even fatalities.

We all have had the experience of struggling with software that is not working as expected and is not providing us feedback as to why. With our code, we can often dig in and figure out the source of the issue, but when closed-source software is lacking feedback, a theoretically trivial issue can take hours or days to solve.

Feedback from software systems comes in many forms; these can be visual, auditory, or physical, such as vibrations. Our IDEs give us instant feedback with syntax highlighting, letting us know with red squiggly lines when some code is problematic. Compilers and interpreters give textual feedback, hopefully letting us know what is wrong with the code, and even sometimes how to fix it.

Ideally, systems should provide detailed, descriptive, and instant feedback informing the user specifically what is wrong and how to fix it.

4.5.2   Familiarity

In Chapter 1, we discussed the importance of familiarity and how it is critical in reducing communication bandwidth and errors. As such, we will only mention it here as a reminder.

4.5.3   Progressive Disclosure

Progressive disclosure of complexity is a design technique that involves revealing information or functionality to the user in a gradual and incremental manner. This is done in order to reduce cognitive overload. In software, progressive disclosure of complexity can be applied in a number of ways, such as:

- Hiding advanced or infrequently used features behind a menu or toggle so that they are only accessible to users who need them.
- Presenting information and options in a step-by-step manner, rather than all at once.
- Providing context-sensitive help or guidance to the user as they work, rather than presenting all the information up front.
- Documentation that explains the high level before going into the details.
- Enabling the usage of default, optional arguments in interfaces such as APIs or functions.

Progressive disclosure of complexity can be particularly useful for applications that have a steep learning curve, or that are intended for use by a wide range of users with different levels of expertise. By gradually revealing more complex features and options as the user becomes more familiar with the application, you improve the product's usability and can help users feel more confident and in control as they learn to use it.

Progressive disclosure is common in the education system. For instance, the various scientific models of the atom are taught to children starting with the simple. I remember in fifth grade or so being taught that electrons orbit the nucleus, and only much later being taught about the more accurate standing wave model.

4.5.4   Explicit vs. Implicit

The Zen of Python (see appendix) is a collection of the nineteen design principles of Python. It is a masterful collection and is relevant to all software projects. I highly recommend you take a look at it.

The second principle states: "Explicit is better than implicit." This principle states that it is better for the code to be explicit in its functionality and constraints rather than relying on implicit, hidden, or assumed behavior. By being explicit, you make it easier for others (and yourself) to understand what your code is doing. Being explicit is communicating; being implicit is not communicating.

In the Rust programming language, functions automatically return their last expression if that expression does not end with a semicolon. For example, in the add function below, the result of a+b is returned. The return keyword is *implicit* in this case.

```
fn add(a: u32, b: u32) -> u32 {
    a + b
}
```

Python requires the return keyword to be explicitly written.

```
def add(a: int, b: int) -> int:
    return a + b
```

Notice that the return keyword is a communication tool; it communicates a computation to human readers. Consider in which language is the function's intended action easier to understand? Which function is less likely to confuse an engineer? Which function is less likely to lead to bugs? Which function has a higher cognitive load? Is it worth saving an engineer a few keystrokes for the costs?

The Ruby programming language is another example of a language that has a confusing implicit syntax. In Ruby, functions can be called without parenthesis. For example, the method compute_something can be called with parenthesis:

```
result = compute_something(parameter1, parameter2)
```

or without parenthesis:

```
results = compute_something parameter1, parameter2
```

That is *not* a typo in the book. That is actually what Ruby code looks like! The compute_something function is implicitly called. The syntax is such that it is not clearly communicating to the reader what is going on. It takes a bit of thinking and background knowledge to figure out what's actually happening. This syntax does not follow the principles of familiarity, in the sense that most engineers are not familiar with a parenthesis-less function call syntax.

You may believe that the syntaxes are only confusing to those who don't know the languages. You may be under the impression that the syntaxes are not inherently confusing. You may think that the Python syntax of using parenthesis and explicit return statements would be confusing to a Ruby or Rust engineer.

This is the wrong way of looking at it. Good design is about reducing the complexity of everything for everyone. The average engineer trained in the average language would find these syntaxes unfamiliar and confusing. Remember that minor complexities add up very quickly and that the improbable occurs.

In fact, I once had to debug an ex-coworker's Ruby code running in production. At the time, I had never even seen Ruby code before. It was insane, the code was crap, and it did not make any sense, because I did not know about Ruby's crazy parenthesis-less syntax. To make matters worse, I was working under pressure, as the broken code was preventing the exporting of a patient's medical records, which urgently needed to be sent to a hospital.

So why would someone design a syntax as strange as Ruby's? What were they thinking? My best guess is that they were under the mind-destroying influence of extremism.

4.6 Avoid Extremism and Fads

> I think programming is a lot like religion; people have their beliefs.
> Some people like to force their beliefs on others.
> — Donald Knuth - Programmers at Work

It's easy to get carried away by a "good idea," especially one that we have come up with ourselves. The creator of Ruby probably thought it was a great idea to not require parenthesis to call functions. He was probably emotionally attached to his idea. He probably thought that it's a great way to make code more elegant and minimalistic, but really, he was deluding himself with self-serving bias.

As Don Norman writes, "Rule of thumb: if you think something is clever and sophisticated beware—it is probably self-indulgence."

Just as there are extremists in the political and religious worlds, there are extremists in the engineering world. And just as extremists inevitably cause harm in the real world, they cause harm in the engineering world.

Extremist engineers are dangerous. Their ideas and opinions should be mostly ignored. Extremists are people who are not level-headed, who don't understand nuance and tradeoffs, and who are blinded by cognitive deficiencies or emotional issues.

Charlie Munger discussed the risks of extremist ideology in one of his famous speeches.

> Another thing I think should be avoided is extremely intense ideology because it cabbages up one's mind.
>
> You've seen that. You see a lot of it on TV you know preachers for instance, you know they've all got different ideas about theology and a lot of them have minds that are made of cabbage.
>
> But that can happen with political ideology. And if you're young it's easy to drift into loyalties and when you announce

that you're a loyal member and you start shouting the or-
thodox ideology out what you're doing is pounding it in,
pounding it in and you're gradually ruining your mind so you
want to be very careful with this ideology. It's a big danger.

In my mind I got a little example I use whenever I think
about ideology and it's these Scandinavian canoeists who
succeeded in taming all the rapids of Scandinavia and they
thought they would tackle the whirlpools in the Aaron Rapids
here in the United States. The death rate was 100whirlpool
is not something you want to go into and I think the same is
true about a really deep ideology.

. . .

But this business of not drifting into extreme ideology is a
very, very important thing in life if you want to have more
correct knowledge and be wiser than other people. A heavy
ideology is very likely to do you in. [12]

Whenever there is a battle between two sides, with extremists on both
sides, it's usually an indication that the truth lies somewhere in between.
The world is nuanced, and humans have a tendency to build mental
models that are simple and lacking in critical nuance. Our minds like to
think about single causes producing single effects, and have a hard time
thinking about all the causes, effects, and second-order effects that exist
in the real world. As a rule, you should not trust non-nuanced opinions
(especially on controversial topics) or adopt extremist ideologies.

4.6.1   Fads

Fads are not as bad as extremism, but they should be treated with caution. Many of the human flaws that lead to extremism also lead to fads.
Everyone wants to use the latest and greatest thing. No one wants to feel
left behind with a technology of the past.

Having decades of experience in engineering gives one perspective on
fads. I have seen so many methodologies, languages, and frameworks

come and go. One day they are the hottest thing and next year they are forgotten. New technologies are often not as good as they appear, the kinks have not been worked out, the deficiencies are not well documented, and the community support is non-existent.

If you decide to implement a long-lifespan project with the latest fad, you might be in trouble when the fad passes. Suddenly the hot framework or language you used is no longer being supported and you need to rewrite your code from scratch.

In general, new technologies and methodologies should be avoided for critical projects until they are proven and sufficiently mature. This will often require years of usage by the engineering community. The primary exception to this rule is that if the new technology can provide a huge advantage over alternative approaches, then it might be worth considering.

4.6.2 Examples of Extremism and Fads

Name	Type	Description
Anti-singletons	Extremism	The belief that singletons are evil in all contexts and should never be used.
Extreme programming (XP)	Fad & extremism	A type of agile development that includes programming in pairs and unit testing of all code. Literally has "extreme" in its name.
Self-documenting code	Extremism	The idea that code should not contain comments and instead be so well written that it is self-documenting.
Test-driven development (TDD)	Fad & extremism	A software development process relying on software requirements being converted to test cases before the code is written.
Aspect-oriented programming	Fad	A programming paradigm that aims to increase modularity by allowing the separation of cross-cutting concerns. [20]
Blockchain	Fad [5]	A type of distributed ledger technology that consists of a growing list of records, called blocks, that are securely linked together using cryptography. [21]
Obsession with efficiency	Extremism	An obsession with the run time complexity of code and a desire to minimize it irrespective of the utility [6].

I could add many more rows to this table, but I don't want to make too many enemies.

If something sounds great in theory but has never been implemented well in practice, you should assume there is something fundamentally flawed with it. If something is popular and old, it's probably pretty good. If something is popular and new, you should hold your judgment and wait it out. Popularity is not a reliable metric for the utility of *new* things.

4.6.3   Follow the Path

There is an Israeli proverb that teaches: "The path is wiser than the one who walks it." The path has been worn down by many people who walked it in the past; if there was a shorter or safer way, then that would have become the path. The optimal paths tend to appear naturally from the footsteps of the masses. The best paths become popular and remain popular, while the less optimal paths fade.

This proverb relates to software development in that it guides engineers and designers to follow proven things instead of following the latest fad or extremism.

The idea is similar to the **efficient market hypothesis,** which states that assets are always correctly priced given that all relevant information is freely and readily available to market participants and is rapidly and accurately incorporated into asset prices. If there was a more correct price for an asset, then that would be its price. The same holds true for paths, if better paths existed they would be the common paths.

In my opinion, the efficient market hypothesis is not a law but rather an approximate model of asset pricing. It is not precise and there are many cases when prices are outright inefficient, as is evident from the fact that it is possible to consistently beat the market, as Warren Buffet and Charlie Munger have been doing for 50+ years.

And just as sometimes the market is not efficient, sometimes it makes sense to follow a fad. Sometimes the masses are correct in their promotion of a fad. For example, object-oriented programming was a fad and is now a recommended practice. So don't become an anti-fad extremist. If you are going to follow a fad, do it with caution and a critical mind.

Chapter 5

Investing in the Right Things

In the introduction, we discussed how software engineering is akin to solving a multidimensional optimization problem. There is a problem that needs a solution, and there exist multiple solutions which meet the requirements. Often it's not all that hard to find a solution that meets the requirements. What *is* hard is finding an optimal solution.

The optimal solution for one project or code base is often not the optimal solution for a different one. The optimal solution with a small budget might be completely different from when a large budget is available. A life-critical system, one where someone dies if the system fails, requires a totally different level of code quality and testing than a web application.

Engineering principles and best practices must always be considered in the context of your project and goals. The context is composed of many parts, including the team, the programming language, budgets, deadlines, scale, expected product lifetime, and the existing code base. The ability to consider the context and come to the correct conclusions is a skill that is needed to be a great engineer. Failure to develop this skill will lead to premature optimization, missed deadlines, high development and maintenance costs, and a slew of other undesirable things. Or said another way, it will lower the probability of achieving your goals.

5.1 Prioritize Your Goals

In order to "invest in the right things," you must first prioritize your objectives. This involves identifying which objectives are most important to your project and estimating the consequences and costs associated with accomplishing and not accomplishing each objective.

If your goal is to acquire users quickly in order to test product–market fit, then code quality is not a priority, as you will probably throw away all your code as you iterate through ideas. In this case, the cost of quality code at present is very high relative to the opportunity cost of releasing a product quickly.

As engineers, we prioritize our goals, often subconsciously. Subconscious prioritization is great if our subconscious prioritizes optimally. But often our subconscious prioritizes the present over the future and must be actively corrected. After all, the present is what is in front of our eyes and the consequences more immediate. This can be considered a form of availability bias.

Availability bias is a cognitive bias that occurs when individuals make decisions based on information that is readily available to them rather than on all of the relevant information. This can lead to inaccurate judgments and poor decisions because people tend to rely on information that is easily accessible and immediate instead of other factors that may be relevant to the decision.

Our focus on the present often leads us to forget our goal of keeping long-term costs low. We are biased to rush to quick and dirty solutions, often leading to outsized costs.

5.2   Tradeoffs

Most of the challenge of optimization comes from the difficulty of comparing tradeoffs. When choosing a system design or even when writing a single line of code, you must always consider the tradeoffs of your design choices. **Tradeoff analysis**, as the name implies, is the process of analyzing the various tradeoffs of a decision. In terms of engineering, it consists of determining and considering the advantages and disadvantages of each engineering choice, including how each choice affects the product and team, both locally and holistically.

Design and engineering require tradeoffs, there is no way around it. There are always tradeoffs. If you are unaware of them, or do not consider them, it is highly unlikely your design will be optimal. Below is a table of the most common tradeoffs that engineers encounter. You can use this table as a tool when performing tradeoff analysis.

More of this	Less of this
Compute efficiency	Readability, maintainability, development costs, simplicity
Security	*
Scalability	*
Cost now	Cost later
Development time now	Development time later
Simplicity	Extensibility
Features	Usability, maintainability, budget remaining
Automatic	User control
Backward compatibility	Simplicity, performance, agility
Faster product to market	Quality, usability, maintainability, readability, performance, reliability

Table 5.1: Common tradeoffs in software development

5.3 Cost Estimation Under Uncertainty

The question arises, how can one compare tradeoffs? How can one know where to compromise and where to be strict? How can one know what the correct balance is for the task at hand?

The tradeoffs are so different that comparing them can feel like comparing apples to oranges. Luckily, there is a method for comparing different things. The way to do it is to translate them into a proxy value and then compare those proxy values. For example, we can compare apples and oranges by how much pleasure we experience from eating them, or by their market values.

For most projects, the proxy value that is best for comparing tradeoffs is monetary value over time. Even if no actual money will be exchanged, monetary value can still be used. For example, on volunteer open-source projects, monetary value can be calculated in terms of engineering time, utility to users, and goodwill.

Computing monetary value is not trivial, and it is made extra difficult due to the unpredictable nature of the world. The world is far too chaotic to know what the outcome of a decision will be. In some cases, a decision may only incur the initial development costs, and in others, it will lead to disaster and the bankrupting of a company.

Of course, since we don't know what will happen in the future, we can't know what the actual costs of each decision will be. What we can do, however, is construct a **probabilistic cost model**, or PCM. A PCM considers a range of possible outcomes, their relative probabilities of occurring, and their individual costs. In expectation, or on average, such a model will provide an accurate estimation of future costs.

A probabilistic cost model consists of multiple cost outcome graphs along with their probability of occurring. In Figure 5.1 is a **cost outcome graph** (COG) of a new feature. In this example, there is the initial development cost, which mostly consists of the engineer's time and morale, and then a small cost at some point in the future related to a bug. The cost of the bug might consist of an engineer's time, loss of productivity, or the loss of a customer.

Things start getting interesting when we consider the probabilistic aspect of PCMs. The graph in Figure 5.1 represents only one of the possible outcomes. There are, of course, many other outcomes that may occur. It is impossible to consider every possible outcome, since there are an infinite number of possible magnitudes for each point in time. Rather, we consider each category of outcome and its probability of occurring. There is the category where things go well, there is the category where disaster strikes, and there is a category of somewhere in between. For each category of outcome, we create a graph that contains the average values of that category.

$$expected\ cost = \sum_{n \in COGs} probability_n \times cost_n$$

Figure 5.2: Probabilistic cost model expected cost equation. Here we sum over the set of possible cost outcomes.

The total cost of a single COG can be calculated by measuring the area under its graph. To calculate the cost of the entire cost model, i.e., the cost of an engineering decision, one must calculate the costs of all the possible outcomes. To do this, one must multiply the area under each COG by its probability of occurring. The sum of this quantity is the expected cost, or average cost, of an engineering decision. Mathematically, this is described in Figure 5.2.

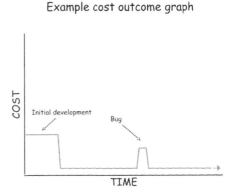

Figure 5.1: Example cost outcome graph of a new feature

Let's look at a few simple examples so you can get a better idea of what PCMs and COGs look like.

A Leaky Roof

Fixing a leak in a roof induces a small cost today, but it will save tens of thousands of dollars in future structural damages. Assuming that the cost to fix the leak is less than the cost to fix the future structural damages, [1]it makes sense to fix the leak today.

Figure 5.3: Fix leaky roof now   Figure 5.4: Fix leaky roof later

Selecting an Automotive Part

A car manufacturer must choose between parts of varying quality. A less expensive part may not cause problems, or it may lead to drivers (users) dying and lawsuits. At present time, it is unknown if the less expensive part will sufficiently stand up to wear or if it will lead to disaster.

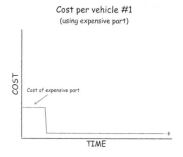
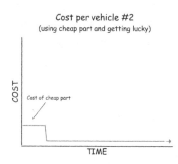

Figure 5.5: Cost per vehicle with the   Figure 5.6: Cost per vehicle with the
expensive part   cheap part

---

[1]More accurately, you want to consider the discounted cost of capital, but since finance is out of scope for this book, let's just keep it simple.

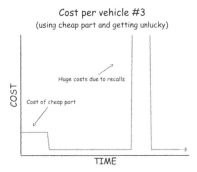

Figure 5.7: Cost per vehicle with the cheap part and a vehicle recall.

Quick and Dirty Software Development

Quick and dirty (Q&D) is a development style where very little time is spent planning, designing, and creating the product. Engineers simply write whatever comes first to their minds without considering the consequences and long-term costs. In Figure 5.8, we see the typical cost outcome graph of Q&D.

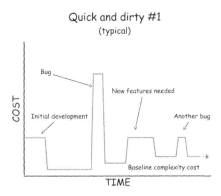

Figure 5.8: Quick and dirty #1. A typical outcome.

As time goes on, bug and new feature costs will appear to the right. Notice how the cost of new features and bugs are more than the initial development costs. Notice that the baseline cost goes from zero to a small value. This is the cost that comes from this feature's complexity increasing the development and maintenance costs of other parts of the project.

Sometimes engineers get lucky and Q&D ends up not being all that expensive. Figure 5.9 represents such a scenario. This type of scenario is more likely to occur on small, low-complexity projects with a single maintainer.

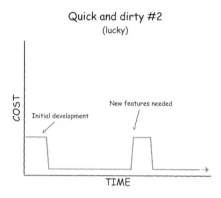

Figure 5.9: Quick and dirty #2. A lucky outcome.

On more complex projects, quick and dirty often turns out to be not so quick and very dirty. If the complexity is too great, then building an initial quick solution will often end up taking longer than attempting a quality solution. In the disaster scenario in Figure 5.10, notice the cost of the bug is off the chart. Unfortunately, this scenario is not that uncommon; bugs like this typically include costs related to lost customers, damage to property, or downtime.

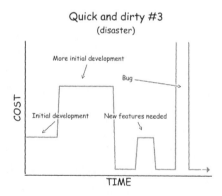

Figure 5.10: Quick and dirty #3. Disaster strikes.

Design and Build Carefully Software Development

This is the scenario where code is designed and written carefully. In Figure 5.11, notice that the initial development costs are slightly larger than in the quick and dirty scenario, but new features and bugs are less expensive. This brings the total cost of this outcome graph to be lower than the quick and dirty scenario #1.

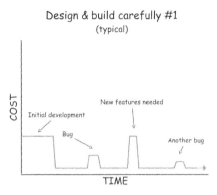

Figure 5.11: Design and build carefully #1. A typical outcome.

Sometimes you get lucky; there are no bugs and all goes smoothly as shown in Figure 5.12. When designing carefully, you are much more likely to "get lucky."

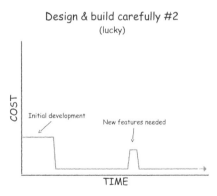

Figure 5.12: Design and build carefully #2. A lucky outcome.

Sometimes, despite your best efforts to design carefully, things go wrong. Even so, when designing carefully, the average magnitude of bad things is lower than when practicing Q&D. Note that the cost of the disaster scenario in Figure 5.13 is much less than the total cost in the quick and dirty disaster scenario.

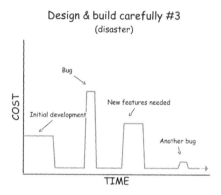

Figure 5.13: Design and build carefully #3. Disaster strikes.

Negative Costs

For simplicity's sake, I have so far not discussed negative costs. In theory, cost outcome graphs should dip into the negative when an outcome is beneficial or profitable. Personally, I find that including negative cost tends to add unnecessary complexity to the model. I believe it is much easier to think about costs and benefits separately. Benefits are less chaotic in nature, and thus, we gain less by modeling them with a PCM. A simple Gaussian distribution or a long-tailed distribution is sufficient for modeling most benefit cases.

Unless you have some uncanny ability to think about negative costs, or the nature of your specific problem requires you to include negative costs in your model, I recommend you calculate the costs and benefits separately.

5.3.1   Pragmatic Probabilistic Cost Modeling

You might be wondering, how is it even possible to generate a single cost outcome graph? How can one know what the correct magnitudes are, or what type of things may go wrong?

To be clear, I am not recommending you actually draw these graphs, estimate their probabilities, and then numerically calculate the expected cost. Rather, I am suggesting that you should use PCMs as a tool for thinking about design and engineering decisions.

Generating even approximately accurate PCMs is not easy, and requires many years of paying attention to outcomes. Of course, even after many years, you will still often err. But fortunately, you don't need to get it perfectly right. Just take your best guess and use ideas such as Jackson's law, Murphy's law, and scale laws, to correct your initial best guess. Your models will probably be good enough.

5.4 The Pareto Principle (The 80/20 Rule)

The **Pareto principle**, also called the 80/20 rule, is a well-known concept in business and economics that states that roughly 80% of effects come from 20% of causes. This principle is relevant in many fields, including software engineering.

The Pareto principle applies to software in many ways. For example, 20% of the code and functionality often provides 80% of the value, or 80% of a project's bugs are caused by 20% of the code.

If you have a limited amount of engineering hours that need to be allocated, then the Pareto principle states that they should be spent on the 20% of code or features that provide 80% of the value. The Pareto principle is a cognitive tool to remind you that not all code and functionality are of equal value. You should use the principle to prioritize your goals, weigh tradeoffs and generate probabilistic cost models.

5.5 Diminishing Returns

The law of diminishing returns is a fundamental concept in economics that states that as additional units of a resource are added to a production process, the marginal output of that resource will eventually decline. In other words, this means that at some point, increasing the amount of a particular resource used in production will not result in a proportional increase in output.

In software engineering, the law of diminishing returns applies in a number of different ways. Adding engineers to a team may initially result in an increase in the rate of code production. However, at some point, the value of each additional engineer will decrease. Eventually, the cost of employing additional engineers begins to outweigh the benefits. Figure 5.14 below demonstrates the point.

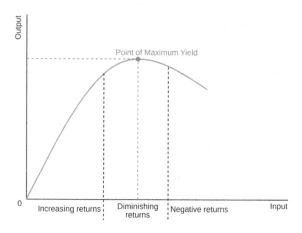

Figure 5.14: Diminishing returns. [2]

Another way in which the law of diminishing returns applies in software engineering is in the optimization of code. As you strive to make code more performant, you may initially see significant improvements from a small amount of effort. However, as you continue to optimize the code, you will find that the marginal gains from additional effort become smaller and smaller. In this case, the law of diminishing returns dictates that there is a point at which the effort invested in further optimization is not justified by the resulting improvements in performance.

Peter Norvig suggests how to deal with the law of diminishing returns in *Coders at Work*.

> There are 100 other things you could be doing that are just at the bottom of the curve where you get much better returns. And at some point you have to say, "Enough is enough, let's stop and go do something where we get a better return." [18]

When deciding where to channel engineering resources, it's crucial to consider the law of diminishing returns. Keeping it in mind helps make more optimal decisions on where to invest limited engineering resources.

5.6 High-Yield investments

The Pareto principle along with the law of diminishing returns teach us that there are certain investments which have a higher yield than others. Let's review the three categories to which most high-yield investments belong.

5.6.1 Lifespan

Investments in products that have a long lifespan will have outsized yields. This is apparent from looking at a PCM of a long-lifespan product. A poor design choice will shift the entire distribution upward. If the product's lifespan is long, then even a minor shift has a large overall effect. In the realm of software, long-lifespan products are typically schemas, interfaces, division of components, names, protocols, specifications, and formats. Consider how long TCP/IP, JPEG, and HTTP have been around. Products which are specifications are particularly long-lived because there are many different implementations of the specification and a large number and variety of users.

There exists a **coordination problem** in changing a specification, i.e., a difficulty in getting all the users and usages to change together. Imagine trying to change TCP/IP—if the change is not backward compatible, you will need to update every router in the world, it's an impossible task! Due to coordination problems, engineers are often required to support multiple versions of products while gradually deprecating old ones. Supporting multiple versions simultaneously is often the only practical approach, but of course, it leads to large additional costs.

It follows that code that has a short lifespan does not need to be invested in as heavily. If you are just writing a script to parse some data which will then be thrown away, it probably does not make sense to be a perfectionist about it. That being said, you must be confident that the code will in fact have a short lifespan. Often, code we think will have a short lifespan lasts for a long, long time.

5.6.2 Scale

Similar to products that have a long lifespan, products that have or will have a large number of users or usages have a high return on investment. The number of usages is a type of "scale" and, thus, abides by the **scale law of returns**discussed earlier.

5.6.3 Foundations

A unit of code or data that is foundational to the system, program, or company should be invested in heavily. Similar to a house, if your foundation is not built well, your whole house will collapse, and all investment in other aspects of the house will be wasted. Foundations typically consist of the system architecture, division of components, schema, and abstractions.

5.7 Premature Optimization

Premature optimization refers to the practice of optimizing a program early in the development process before it's been proven to be necessary.

Inexperienced engineers, especially those coming out of universities, often over-prioritize the importance of performance optimization. This is probably because computer science programs tend to overemphasize and fetishize time complexity. This fetish is unfortunately contagious and gets passed to the next generation of CS students.

Donald Knuth famously stated that "Premature Optimization is the root of all evil (or at least most of it)." Knuth's statement is a bit extreme in my opinion, but the point remains. Premature optimization is very bad. Let's review some of the reasons:

- It is easy for an engineer to waste tons of time obsessing about making a unit of code faster. Optimization is a never-ending process;

there is always more efficiency that can be squeezed out of the code, but the returns are diminishing.

- Code is likely to be thrown away or changed. Investing in optimizing a function that will soon be discarded is wasteful.

- Most code does not need to be optimized. It is already fast enough.

- Performance-optimized code is usually much harder to understand and maintain. It is more likely to contain bugs and increases engineering costs.

Bernie Cosell, one the one of pioneering engineers of the internet, said:

> ... students get too clever by half, 'This is the ideal place to do an AB unbalanced 2-3 double reverse backwards pointer cube thing and I always wanted to write one of those'. So they spend a week or two tuning an obscure part of a program that doesn't need anything. [18]

As Don Norman says in *The Design of Everyday Things*,

> Rule of thumb: if you think something is clever and sophisticated beware—it is probably self-indulgence. [15]

It's generally better to wait until you have collected data and identified actual performance bottlenecks before trying to optimize your code. Write your code as lucidly, simply, and clearly as you can. And then, if it needs to be sped up later, you can optimize it later. In general, it's better to pick a design that fits your data and mental models than the one that is the fastest. Don't fall for the temptation to show off how smart you are by implementing the "double reverse backwards pointer thing;" it will just waste your and your co-worker's time. And if your co-workers are worth their salt, they won't be impressed by your "ingenuity;" they will think you are a noob.

5.8   Featuritis

Knuth believes that premature optimization is the root of all evil, but I think featuritis is a greater evil.

Featuritis is a term used to describe a situation in which a product has too many features, making it overly complex, difficult to use, and hard to maintain. Featuritis often occurs over time as users request additional features and engineers and product managers fail to say "no." **Feature creep**, which is the process that most often leads to featuritis, describes the phenomenon of features slowly creeping into a product over time.

Users, product managers, and even engineers are often under the delusion that more features are better. The main issue with too many features is that it makes products too complex. As Don Norman writes:

> "Complexity probably increases as the square of the features: double the number of features, quadruple the complexity. Provide ten times as many features, multiply the complexity by one hundred." [15]

Apple is famous for successfully fighting feature creep. On the iPhone, for example, many basic features are not supported. Users can't add more than four items to the dock, icons can only be placed at specific locations on the home screen (they are snapped into place), and icon sizes cannot be modified. Limitations like these reduce the complexity of the interface and make iOS a more usable product for most users. It can be argued that much of Apple's success comes from its obsession with reducing complexity.

Besides negatively impacting the user experience, featuritis impacts the engineering experience. Software with many features is very difficult to maintain and improve. Features are rarely standalone; every feature depends on something else, such as state information, protocols, APIs, or other features. The existence of a feature, thus, restricts changes to its dependencies. If you want to change an API, for example, then you will need to change all the features that depend on that API.

The idea that adding more features does not increase the utility of a product is often called "**worse is better**". At a certain point, having less functionality ("worse") becomes the more desirable choice ("better"). Software that is limited in functionality and, thus, complexity, is often more appealing to the users than the opposite.

5.8.1   Preventing Featuritis

When receiving a request for a new feature, the first thing to ask yourself is if it's worth implementing. Does the value provided by the feature outweigh the costs? The costs you need to consider include usability, initial development costs, maintenance costs, and complexity costs.

If you determine that the feature is not worth implementing, just say "no." Saying "no" *is* part of your job as an engineer. You were not hired to be a feature monkey and destroy the code base with featuritis. You were hired to help the company achieve its goals, and saying "no" is often the best way to do that.

Jeff Geerling writes in an article titled "Just say no" that as an engineer, you should "Be liberal with your 'no', be judicious with your 'yes'." [6]

Another way to prevent featuritis is to remove features periodically. Every few months, I usually get frustrated at the code base and look for features, functions, and files to remove. Sometimes it bothers my co-workers when they get a message from me letting them know I want to delete their code. Overall, as long as I don't get too carried away, they appreciate it, as I clean up their trash for them.

5.9   Over-Engineering

Over-engineering in software development refers to the practice of creating overly complex and unnecessary solutions to problems. This can occur when engineers implement excessive or unnecessary features, use unnecessarily advanced technologies, design overly complex architectures, or use excessive abstraction.

The tweet in Figure 5.15 is a great example of over-engineering.

Figure 5.15: Over-engineering tweet [17]

Stack Overflow is one of the most popular websites in the world, receiving tens of millions of page views per day. A product like Stack Overflow must have high availability and be able to deal with massive amounts of traffic. Stack Overflow is not a trivial application; it has a bunch of functionality, insane traffic, and a huge amount of data. ByteByteGo created a great graphic (Figure 5.16 that uses Stack Overflow's architecture as an example to demonstrate engineers' propensity for over-engineering.

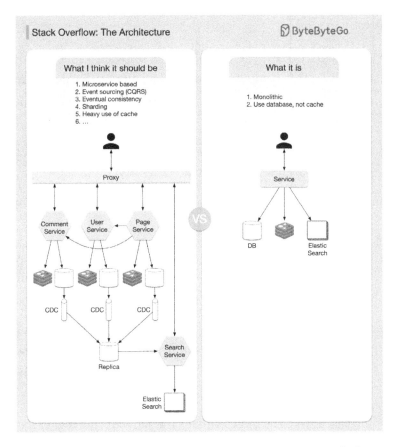

Figure 5.16: Stack Overflow architecture from ByteByteGo [19]

In my many years of engineering, I have seen over-engineering happen again and again. In fact, I think over-engineering is more common than proper engineering. It seems like it is the default choice for most engineers. Engineers are often blind to their own over-engineering, either because they have not been able to come up with a simpler solution or because they are affected by self-serving bias. It is sexier to build a big complex system like the one on the left than a simple app with a database like the one on the right. At most organizations, the one on the left is considered more impressive and more likely to lead to a promotion.

While it may seem like a good idea to future-proof a product or cover all possible use cases, over-engineering can have several negative consequences:

- Increased complexity: Over-engineered software is inherently more complex. This complexity makes the software harder to understand, which in turn makes it harder to create, maintain, debug, and update.

- Wasted resources: Over-engineering consumes more resources (engineering time and compute) than necessary.

- Decreased agility: Over-engineered software is less adaptable to changes.

- Delayed time to market: Over-engineering often leads to delays in the release of the product, as the unnecessary features and complex solutions take more time to develop and test.

- Poor user experience: Over-engineered software can lead to poor user experience. Unnecessary features can confuse users, and overly complex solutions can slow down the software or make it less reliable.

- Increased risk: The more complex the software, the higher the risk of bugs and security vulnerabilities. It's harder to test and ensure the correctness of overly complex systems.

Extreme programming introduced the catchy phrase **"You Aren't Gonna Need It"** (YAGNI), which advises engineers not to invest in functionality, complexity, or optimizations until it is deemed necessary.

5.10   Minimalism

Minimalism is an excellent antidote to over-engineering, featuritis, and complexity. As an engineer, you should strive for minimalism in your products. To be clear, minimalism does not mean neglecting to write comments, documentation, or using short variable names. Rather, minimalism means not using the big fancy thing if the simple thing will do.

Not using bloated frameworks, third-party libraries, and complicated design patterns. It means not adding extra features, compilation processes, or abstractions unless there is a *strong* justification for them. When your code is more minimalistic, there are fewer things that can go wrong, fewer things to be confused by, and fewer things in the way of progress.

The principle of minimalism applies to the non-software world as well. When traveling, the more luggage you have, the more difficult and more expensive it is to move around. The more cars you have, the more garages you need, the more property tax you need to pay, and the more oil changes and emissions tests you need to be burdened with. As we can see, there are second-order effects to bloat. Minimalism is a great way to automatically avoid them.

Figure 5.17: XKCD The General Problem #974

When I interview frontend engineers, I ask them to build a web page that consists of a few buttons, and some text that is to be displayed depending on the timing of when the buttons are clicked. I won't get into all the details, but it's not that complex. When done properly, the whole thing requires maybe 25 lines of plain old JavaScript and a few HTML elements. In my experience, 90% of the candidates, those that have already passed an initial phone screen, end up failing this assignment.

I let the engineers use whatever tools, frameworks, and languages they want; they are allowed to use Google, Stack Overflow, etc. Most engineers choose to use a bulky frontend framework; some choose to use TypeScript, and then build scripts to transpile the TypeScript to JavaScript. Others use a boilerplate template complete with Node.js and all the various build and deploy configurations. These engineers nearly always fail. They get stuck installing packages, getting their configurations to work, fixing URL routing issues, etc. If they do succeed in getting all the bloat to work, often there is a bug in the functionality, i.e., the buttons don't function in the way that I had asked for. Often, this is because the bloat has added complexity, making the functionality harder to implement, or because they have spent so much time setting everything up that they did not have time to invest in the functionality.

I have consistently found that the candidates that choose a minimalistic approach tend to have a much higher success rate in meeting the requirements and achieving the desired functionality. Of course, this anecdote generalizes to all engineering problems. Minimalism is a powerful practice that helps engineers achieve their objectives.

5.11 The Middle Way

The **middle way**, also known as the **golden mean**, is the idea that the optimal path is the one in the middle between two extremes. Or in other words, that the optimal path is the path of moderation. The middle way has a long history, and can be found in philosophical and religious teachings from all over the world. The ancient Greek philosophers, such as Plato, Socrates, and Aristotle recommend following the middle way. Scholars from many of the world's religions, such as Judaism, Islam, and Buddhism have encouraged their practitioners to take the middle way.

The middle way applies not only to religion but also to engineering. It is a great heuristic for guiding engineering decisions.

In the book *Surely You're Joking, Mr. Feynman!* [4], Feynman retells a story of using the middle way to select gears for a mechanical computer. During WWII, before he worked on the Manhattan Project, Feynman was assigned to building mechanical computers for calculating artillery trajectories. The computers consisted of many interconnected gears which would turn to perform calculations. Feynman's manager gave him the following advice on how to select gears.

> There are two rules you need to know to design these machines. First, the friction in every bearing is so-and-so much, and in every gear junction, so-and-so much. From that, you

can figure out how much force you need to drive the thing.

Second, when you have a gear ratio, say 2 to 1, and you are wondering whether you should make it 10 to 5 or 24 to 12 or 48 to 24, here's how to decide: You look in the Boston Gear Catalog, and select those gears that are in the middle of the list. The ones at the high end have so many teeth they're hard to make, if they could make gears with even finer teeth, they'd have made the list go even higher. The gears at the low end of the list have so few teeth they break easy. So the best design uses gears from the middle of the list. [4]

In this story, we see the power of the middle way. Even without knowledge of the gears' physical properties, the middle way enabled Feynman to make good engineering decisions.

The middle way is a great anecdote to extremism, over-engineering, premature optimization, featuritis, and many other bad engineering practices.

5.12 Worse Is Better

Worse is better (WIB) is not only about featuritis, but is rather a general approach to code and software. In the original 1989 WIB essay by Richard Gabriel he contrasted the WIB approach to the MIT approach [26].

Here is what he wrote about the two approaches.

The MIT approach

- Simplicity—the design must be simple, both in implementation and interface. It is more important for the interface to be simple than the implementation.

- Correctness—the design must be correct in all observable aspects. Incorrectness is simply not allowed.

- Consistency—the design must not be inconsistent. A

design is allowed to be slightly less simple and less complete to avoid inconsistency. Consistency is as important as correctness.

- Completeness—the design must cover as many important situations as is practical. All reasonably expected cases must be covered. Simplicity is not allowed to overly reduce completeness.

The worse is better approach

- Simplicity—the design must be simple, both in implementation and interface. It is more important for the implementation to be simple than the interface. Simplicity is the most important consideration in a design.

- Correctness—the design must be correct in all observable aspects. It is slightly better to be simple than correct.

- Consistency—the design must not be overly inconsistent. Consistency can be sacrificed for simplicity in some cases, but it is better to drop those parts of the design that deal with less common circumstances than to introduce either implementational complexity or inconsistency.

- Completeness—the design must cover as many important situations as is practical. All reasonably expected cases should be covered. Completeness can be sacrificed in favor of any other quality. In fact, completeness must be sacrificed whenever implementation simplicity is jeopardized. Consistency can be sacrificed to achieve completeness if simplicity is retained; especially worthless is consistency of interface.

To summarize the worse is better approach: simplicity is of primary importance and all should be sacrificed for it.

Let's step back for a second, and consider why there was disagreement between the MIT and Bell Labs engineering teams. How can two groups of talented and brilliant engineers come to opposing conclusions? Maybe there are two ways to the optimal solution? Or maybe one team was simply wrong?

There are probably many partially correct answers as to why the two teams disagreed. One answer is that biases, groupthink, and familiarity led the teams to diverge into different development styles. Another answer is that the teams had different goals, different users, and different resources. Maybe MIT had more students and inexperienced engineers using the interfaces, so it was critical that the interfaces be as simple as possible. Maybe Bell Labs, a more commercial entity, had strict deadlines and needed to get things to work quickly to meet deadlines, so implementation simplicity was prioritized over correctness and interfaces.

Yet again, we see how engineering choices should take context into consideration. When you find yourself being exposed to an engineering dogma, consider in what contexts (if any) does the dogma make sense.

Personally, I think that both MIT and Bell Labs are justified in their position on interfaces versus implementation. On projects where there are many interfaces and those interfaces are widely used, then making sure those are simple is the priority. On projects that are small, maybe personal projects, a simple implementation may be a better choice as it may not be worthwhile investing in simplifying the interfaces at the cost of complicating the implementation. If you are the only one working on the code base, it's not a problem for you to deal with slightly clunky interfaces, since you are the creator and most likely understand how to use them.

For most cases, I believe worse is better is preferable. It is better to trade off correctness, consistency, and completeness for simplicity. [2]

---

[2]It should be noted that consistency does lead to simplicity. Consistent things have fewer details, and are easier to compress. This is the main reason that consistency is a good practice!

5.13   Sometimes the Wrong Thing Is Right

Voltaire famously wrote that "Perfect is the enemy of good." Voltaire believed that an insistence on achieving perfection often prevents one from accomplishing things that are good. Trying to create a perfect product will prevent you from ever releasing a good product.

Seeking perfection is like attempting to travel at the speed of light; it is an impossibility. Traveling at the speed of light and achieving perfection both require infinite energy. What is the point, when 99% of the speed of light is almost as good and requires a finite amount of energy?

Most books on software engineering preach that an engineer should always do the right thing. They preach an ideology, which is rarely nuanced. Maybe they claim that technical debt should never be accumulated or that all complexity must be eliminated, or singletons are always bad. That the "wrong thing" should never be done. I am not an extremist. I believe that breaking a convention or doing a weird unexpected thing is sometimes better than the alternative. Sometimes using a tool in a way it is not meant to be used is the optimal way to achieve your goals.

Being a great engineer requires you to keep your mind open and consider the taboo, be iconoclastic, and do not fall prey to mind-destroying dogma and extremism.

Chapter 6

Be a Mensch

In the introduction, I discussed how software engineering is a tool for achieving your goals. If one of your goals is to live a fulfilled, meaningful life, then you should follow the practice of being a mensch. And even if you don't care about the quality of your life and just want to be a better engineer, embracing the principles of being a mensch will help you with that as well.

A **mensch** is a Yiddish word that refers to a person of integrity and honor. The term describes someone who is reliable, kind, responsible, and who always does the right thing even when no one is watching. It is a term that is used to show respect and admiration for someone who is truly good at heart. A mensch is someone who takes care of their sick friends, who lets the cashier know when they have returned too much change, and who helps clean up after a party. It is a serious honor to be called a mensch and is not a term that is to be used lightly.

Being a mensch will not only elevates your products, but also your life. Others will be drawn to collaborate with you and entrust you with greater responsibilities. Colleagues will mirror that same integrity back towards you. Doors will be opened for you. You will earn respect and admiration and make the world a better place. Being a mensch will lead you to a happier, more meaningful, and more joyous life.

A mensch is someone who is characterized by:

- Always being honest and truthful, even when it may be difficult.

- Going out of their way to help others, even when it may not be convenient for them.

- Treating others with kindness and respect, even if they are not kind in return.

- Being reliable and dependable and following through on commitments.

- Being humble and not seeking credit or attention for good deeds.

- Being forgiving and understanding, and not holding grudges.

- Taking responsibility for actions, and being accountable for mistakes.

- Considering the effects of their actions on others.

In order to be a mensch you must be hyper-aware of how your actions affect others. You may think that this only includes the people you directly interact with such as your friends, co-workers, or the barista behind the counter, but that is incorrect. Being a mensch also requires you to consider the people you indirectly interact with, such as the users of your products.

Let's consider some of the most important ways in which being a mensch applies to software engineering.

Go Out of Your Way for Others

Go out of your way to be considerate to other engineers. Take the extra minute to make your code easier to understand and more readable. Spend extra effort to document and comment your code clearly. Build your interfaces so that they are not only convenient for your needs but also for the other engineers who will need to interact with them in the present and the future. Consider the curse of knowledge and the curse of cognition in your designs. Go the extra mile to make sure your designs and code are accessible and cultivate empathy for all the engineers and end-users of your products.

Give the Benefit of the Doubt

Giving the benefit of the doubt and making an effort to not succumb to the fundamental attribution bias is imperative to being both a great engineer and mensch. As we discussed in Section 4.1.3, it's best to not jump to conclusions and assume another person's code is garbage or that another engineer is incompetent or lazy. One must withhold judgment until one understands the context in which the code was written.

Don't Leave a Mess

It is not mensch-like to pollute a code base with low-quality code. An engineer who intentionally cuts corners out of laziness or arrogance is being inconsiderate to his fellow engineers. It is the equivalent of leaving a dirty mess in the kitchen of a shared home. Even if your code is part of some module that is only owned by you, you should assume that at some point, someone else will need to look at it.

Internalize Externalities

You should strive to **internalize externalities**. Externalities are things that don't directly affect you. For example, the headaches and inconveniences to users that are caused by your engineering. Internalizing these externalities means acting in a way as if the effects on others are effects on yourself.

This is especially important in products which are deployed at a large scale where individual instances of externalities must be multiplied by their scale. In products that have a large number of users, there is a huge asymmetry between the power of the engineers and that of the users. A little extra effort by the engineer can reap much benefit to the users. A bit of laziness by the engineer can cause many people to be annoyed, suffer, and in some extreme cases even die. In the cases of scale, being a mensch is even more critical.

6.1   Being a Mensch

Being a mensch transcends merely being a "good person." It's a deeper commitment to universal human values, ethical behavior, and genuine respect for others. When you embody the qualities of a mensch, it has a ripple effect, touching every aspect of your products, your life, and the lives of those around you.

Being a mensch benefits you just as much as it benefits those around you. When you display mensch-like qualities, it often encourages others to do the same, creating a virtuous cycle. People will start reflecting your values back to you, building a culture of mutual respect and integrity. The trust you garner will lead to you being entrusted with more responsibilities. Collaborations will become more frequent and fruitful. Opportunities will present themselves more frequently. Doors that once seemed closed or inaccessible will open.

Being a mensch is not merely an external label but a deeply internalized philosophy of life. It guides your actions, decisions, and relationships. And in doing so, it paves the way for a life that is richer in happiness, meaning, and joy. Embracing this path not only benefits you and your products, but also makes the world a better place.

Chapter 7

Wrapping up Book I

In the large and complex world of engineering, it's easy to lose focus and become lost in fads, ideologies, approaches, and misguided optimizations. It is critical to remember that these are just means to an end. It is critical to remember that engineering itself is just a means to an end, and that end is always a human goal. To be effective engineers, we must strive to keep these goals, our terminal objectives, in mind and not get lost in the many distractions along the way.

We must remember that at the core of engineering, at the core of every product— be it a physical item, an application, or a line of code—lies its ultimate recipient: a human being.

Thus, in order to build great products, it is paramount that we don't merely view our work through the lens of functionality, efficiency, or profit. Rather, we must also consider the human element and the entire human–product system in all our engineering and design choices. We must have in mind the people who will use, rely on, and be affected by our choices. We must remember their needs, their moods, their strengths, their shortcomings, and their cognitive diversity.

Neglecting the human dimension is a significant oversight. It's more than just an omission of empathy; it represents a lapse in the very essence of good engineering. Designs that fail to consider their users are inherently flawed.

In our pursuit of excellence, let us remember that the best engineering solutions are those that take into account the bigger picture, our goals, and those that harmonize engineering with the human element.

Postscript

Thanks for reading! I hope you enjoyed this book and learned something valuable.

Book II of the series will be focused on techniques for implementing the theory discussed so far. Unlike this book, Book II is code-heavy and filled with examples. Book II is a work in progress and will likely consist of the following chapters

- Chapter 1: Core Design Techniques

- Chapter 2: Reducing Complexity

- Chapter 3: Defensive Programming

- Chapter 4: Case Studies

- Chapter 5: Testing

- Chapter 6: The Writing Process

- Chapter 7: Maintaining Code

- Chapter 8: The Code Review Checklist

Leave a Review

Thank you for joining me on this journey! If you enjoyed reading, please consider leaving a review. Your feedback is not only immensely valuable to me as an author, but it also helps other readers find this book. Share your thoughts and let others know what you think. You can leave a review on Amazon or Goodreads.com.

Feedback

If you have feedback feel free to email me at zohar@codeisforhumans.com. I would love to receive engineering stories and educational examples that could be used in the next edition or Book II.

Stay Updated

You can join the newsletter to receive updates as chapters are updated and released. Sign up at codeisforhumans.com.

Appendix

1 The Zen of Python

Long-time Pythoneer Tim Peters succinctly channels the BDFL's guiding principles for Python's design into 20 aphorisms, only 19 of which have been written down.

Beautiful is better than ugly.

Explicit is better than implicit.

Simple is better than complex.

Complex is better than complicated.

Flat is better than nested.

Sparse is better than dense.

Readability counts.

Special cases aren't special enough to break the rules.

Although practicality beats purity.

Errors should never pass silently.

Unless explicitly silenced.

In the face of ambiguity, refuse the temptation to guess.

There should be one– and preferably only one –obvious way to do it.

Although that way may not be obvious at first unless you're Dutch.

Now is better than never.

Although never is often better than *right* now.

If the implementation is hard to explain, it's a bad idea.

If the implementation is easy to explain, it may be a good idea.

Namespaces are one honking great idea – let's do more of those!

The Zen of Python is included in Python as an Easter Egg. You can run the following in a Python interpreter:

```
>>> import this
```

List of Figures

List of Tables

Bibliography

[1] Guillaume Alain and Yoshua Bengio. Understanding intermediate layers using linear classifier probes. `https://arxiv.org/pdf/1610.01644.pdf/`, 2018.

[2] Wikimedia Commons. File:diminishing returns graph.svg — wikimedia commons, the free media repository, 2023.

[3] @dorey. Javascript equality table. `https://github.com/dorey/Javascript-Equality-Table/`, 2022.

[4] Richard Feynman. *Surely You're Joking Mr. Feynman!* 1997.

[5] Dr. David Geddes. Advice from nhs to practices affected by qrisk2 it error. *Pulse*, 2016.

[6] Jeff Geerling. Just say no. `https://www.jeffgeerling.com/blog/2022/just-say-no`, 2022.

[7] Richard Hamming. *The Art of Doing Science and Engineering.* 2020.

[8] Yossi (@YossiKreinin) Kreinin. `https://twitter.com/YossiKreinin/status/1590682951691698176`, 1999.

[9] Rob Landley. Understanding the bin, sbin, usr/bin , usr/sbin split. `http://lists.busybox.net/pipermail/busybox/2010-December/074114.html`, 2010.

[10] Donella H. Meadows. *Thinking in Systems.* 2008.

[11] Charlie Munger. Psychology of human misjudgment. `https://fs.blog/great-talks/psychology-human-misjudgment/`.

[12] Charlie Munger. 2007 usc law school commencement address. `https://www.youtube.com/watch?v=jY1eNlL6NKs`, 2007.

[13] Ann Murphy. Calls for action on vacant housing with just 716 homes for rent across the country. *Irish Examiner*, 2022.

[14] D.G Myers. *Exploring Social Psychology, 7th Edition*. 2015.

[15] Donald Norman. *The Design of Everyday Things*. 1988.

[16] Oraguy. Untitled. `https://news.ycombinator.com/item?id=18442637`, 2018.

[17] @ProgrammerHumor. `https://twitter.com/PROGRAMMERHUMOR/status/1514377921636577287?s=20&t=F4o1CICPD_1TuUDMHFHF1A`, 2022.

[18] Peter Seibel. *Coders at Work*. 2009.

[19] Theresa. Ep27: Stack overflow architecture. `https://blog.bytebytego.com/p/ep27-stack-overflow-architecture`, 2022.

[20] Wikipedia. Aspect-oriented programming — Wikipedia, the free encyclopedia. `http://en.wikipedia.org/w/index.php?title=Aspect-oriented%20programming&oldid=1168973337`, 2023.

[21] Wikipedia. Blockchain — Wikipedia, the free encyclopedia. `http://en.wikipedia.org/w/index.php?title=Blockchain&oldid=1169628033`, 2023.

[22] Wikipedia. Broken windows theory — Wikipedia, the free encyclopedia. `http://en.wikipedia.org/w/index.php?title=Broken%20windows%20theory&oldid=1171069975`, 2023.

[23] Wikipedia. Kolmogorov complexity — Wikipedia, the free encyclopedia. `http://en.wikipedia.org/w/index.php?title=Kolmogorov%20complexity&oldid=1171617849`, 2023. [Online; accessed 22-November-2023].

[24] Wikipedia. Numeric keypad — Wikipedia, the free encyclopedia. `http://en.wikipedia.org/w/index.php?title=Numeric%20keypad&oldid=1157351938`, 2023.

[25] Wikipedia. Scope neglect — Wikipedia, the free encyclopedia. http://en.wikipedia.org/w/index.php?title=Scope%20neglect&oldid=1170913215, 2023.

[26] Wikipedia. Worse is better — Wikipedia, the free encyclopedia. http://en.wikipedia.org/w/index.php?title=Worse%20is%20better&oldid=1162705012, 2023.

[27] James Q. Wilson and George L. Kelling. Broken windows. *The Atlantic*, 1982.

[28] Jean Wimmerlin. Shallow focus photography of lion at the wildlife. https://unsplash.com/photos/FC4GY9nQuuO, 2018.

[29] Hyrum Wright. Hyrum's law. https://www.hyrumslaw.com/.

About the Author

Zohar Jackson served as a Software Architect at Mobileye (Israel's top tech company) and Vice President of Engineering at Visionary.ai. Over twenty years of writing software has led him to work on a large variety of software, including self-driving cars, web applications, automated trading for financial firms, computational photography, machine learning, and distributed systems.

Index

Made in the USA
Las Vegas, NV
17 March 2024

87303848R00085